MEM
OF
MALADJUSTED
TEACHER

FROM POSH BOY TO PLEB

NICK YAPP

ISBN 978-1-912145-21-8

Acorn Independent Press

1

In the spring of 1971, I ran away from school. I was 32 years old, and had been a teacher for ten years.

I ran all the way from the nasty school in Wandsworth, where I had been teaching for one long miserable year, to Clapham Junction, and took a train to Waterloo. From Waterloo, I ran to County Hall, then headquarters of the Inner London Education Authority. The person I was desperate to see, the only person in the world I didn't mind calling me 'Nicky', and the person who'd been kind to me when I'd been on one of her courses, was Mary Evans, Inspector for Special Education. Luckily, she was in her office.

I burst in, unheralded. "Mrs Evans," I said, "I don't like Beulah Park School. I don't like Mr Winters, who's Head of the Remedial Department and cuts the children's pencils in half so it takes them twice as long to lose one whole pencil. I don't want to teach there."

Mary was wonderful. "There, there, Nicky," she said. "You shan't work there any longer. You shall go to a new school that's opening this September… a *special* school, a purpose-built school for maladjusted children. It's called New Riverside."

And that was it. No application form, no CV, no interview. I was appointed. Running away had worked.

A couple of weeks later, I received a surprise home visit early one Friday evening from Miriam Daniels, my future Head at New Riverside. Miriam was small, dark, bright-eyed and eager. I later discovered that she was prone to bouts of great energy, and I do mean 'bouts' - especially when enraged.

She professed a love of teaching, though like so many Heads, she seldom indulged this passion. As we sipped coffee, she poured out her plans and her philosophy for the school. There would be outings, cultural activities, cross-curricular time-tabling, and multi-disciplinary case conferences. We should have psychiatrists and psycho-therapists and social workers and psychologists.

"And, of course," said Miriam, "the school will be run on psycho-dynamic lines."

The next step was to meet the newly-appointed staff of New Riverside. We all met to take tea at Miriam's neat house in south-east London. There were four of us - Miriam, Steve Foster (the Deputy Head), Ruby Brinn (the other Class teacher), and me. There were egg sandwiches and sausage rolls, and tea or coffee, and there was learned talk about EPs, Tutorial Units, and someone called Dr Oxshott. Miriam went through the medical and educational reports on children already selected for the school. She had fistfuls of dossiers containing alarming information on these children, in which there was much mention of damage and deprivation, aggression and aberrance, mayhem and madness. I didn't like the sound of what little I could understand, but my abiding memories of that afternoon were those of Ruby (sitting at the wheel of her A35 van, with the evening sun catching her long, golden hair) and of my own feeling of great joy that I had taken the job. Ruby's abiding memory is of the moment when I offered her a sausage roll. I had slipped into the role of waiter at the tea-party, a role that I tend to adopt on social occasions where I don't know anyone present. It's a kind of social running-away, for you become sort of invisible.

I spent the next week torn between joy at the thought of leaving Beulah Park, and extreme anxiety because 'psycho-dynamic' sounded like something out of a Fritz Lang film.

I read the few books that were relevant and discovered that the Special Education world of problem children was split into two rival camps: the Psycho-Dynamic Gang and the Behaviour Modification Mob. The Psycho-Dynamic Gang believed that these maladjusted children would never improve until someone unravelled the mess they were in and helped them gain some insight into the reasons why they found life so appalling. The Behaviour Modification Mob believed that maladjusted children would never improve until their unacceptable behaviour had been so ruthlessly ignored that it withered away. On the side lines stood educational administrators, who simply believed that maladjusted children would never improve.

The Gang and the Mob hated each other and behaved exactly like maladjusted children. On the whole, academic research into the rival systems favoured Behaviour Modification, because the proponents of Behaviour Modification were wickedly skilled at constructing and recording experiments which appeared to alter the behaviour of a maladjusted child, while the proponents of the Psycho-Dynamic School were so dynamic they couldn't construct any experiments at all, let alone make a statistical analysis of what they'd done.

But I knew none of this in the summer holidays when I drove out to the fringes of Inner London Education Authority territory, where the fag end of Lewisham met toffee-nosed Bromley, to see what New Riverside looked like.

It was said that three architects worked on the design of New Riverside, and that two of them had nervous breakdowns in the process. The overall design of the school owed much to Post- Modernist Lunacy. It was a modern, single-storey building, frantically irregular in shape, all angles and corners and juttings-out and tucked-away recesses - a nightmare to police and a joy to any child bent on destroying the fragile working of the school. The exterior walls were of breeze block, faced with a dull red brick; the interior walls were of what was called 'soft cement blocks'. There were huge, fragile windows everywhere, which made you feel that you were teaching in one of Selfridge's shop windows. The first reaction of any child who was distressed was to hurl the nearest thing to hand at the nearest window to hand. This dangerous and expensive state of affairs didn't come to an end until the ILEA installed what were called 'unbreakable' plastic windows some five years later. We never told the children of the change, for by then we had all witnessed the challenge that the word 'unbreakable' issued to them. It took less than a week for an entire box of rulers labelled UNBREAKABLE to become a much bigger box of fragments.

The roof of the school was flat and low. Only the very smallest children couldn't shin up one of the plastic drainpipes in seconds. Once up there, they could spit on us, mock us, bombard us. Over the next seventeen years I spent much of my time warning the children that the roof was flimsy and dangerous, that they could easily fall through, and that they would be horribly injured if they did. Some of this was true, for the mad architects had designed walls so weak that they couldn't support a roof made of traditional materials. So the roof was constructed like an institutional trifle - with a layer of compacted wood shavings dipped in cement, a layer of de-hydrated clay balls on top of this, and a final top layer of tarpaulin, coated with what was supposed to be a waterproof compound. It didn't work. They might as well have topped the whole thing off with custard and flaked almonds, like a proper trifle. In the end, we grew to look forward to the annual visit of The Man with the Bucket of Waterproofing Compound - even though we knew his efforts would be in vain.

The south side of the school contained the five classrooms (one of which was a walkway through to its neighbouring classroom), each with an inner and outer door, so that the children had two escape routes and it was impossible for a teacher to guard both at the same time. This side of the school faced the road, allowing nosey passers-by an excellent view of all that was going on. After a few months, ILEA gardeners planted a row of shrubs, which we hoped would give us privacy as it grew and matured, but every year the same gardeners returned to prune every shrub to almost ground level. We never had any privacy. The narrow east side of the school was home to the Art and Craft room, generous in size, but crepuscular and gloomy in atmosphere. The north side was taken up by the octagonal Hall/Gymnasium, the School Kitchen, the Medical Room, and what I later learned was the Psychiatric Wing. The west side contained the School Office, Miriam's room, the Deputy Head's tiny cell, and the staffroom. At the heart of the building were the children's toilets.

On that first visit, I gazed at my future educational home, in the middle of a vast LCC estate, built in the 1920s. Whatever happened in school would be very much on public display, and I had always felt the need to hide my teaching efforts.

And so the summer of 1971 sped by, as all summers do. September came, and I reported for my first week's work as an officially maladjusted teacher.

There were as yet no pupils in attendance at New Riverside, so that first week was spent holding meetings, unpacking stock, arranging our classrooms, and getting to know each other. Miriam, Steve and Ruby knew all about Special Education. They knew what the initials EWO and SE2 and PSW meant. I hadn't a clue. They knew about maladjusted children. I didn't. All I knew was that a colleague of mine

7

had once visited a maladjusted school and had been struck on the back of the head with a shovel within five minutes of arrival. Unpacking the stock was a delightful experience, and I realised how much better a school works without children, but it was a bit like the Phoney War or Waiting-To-Go-Over-The-Top.

There were more discussions about the children who would be coming to New Riverside. There was much talk of 'psychoses' and 'neuroses', of 'pathologies' and 'sibling rivalries', of 'milestones' and 'dysfunctions'. I tried to pick it up as I went along. The bits I did understand increased my nervousness. The children I would be teaching had, among other things, slashed their arms, extracted their own teeth, tried to commit suicide, and had been thrown out of proper schools for repeated violence. In ten years of teaching, I had never met an officially maladjusted child. Now, I had entered a school that would eventually be full of them.

That process was expected to take several weeks, for Miriam had decided that we would admit only a few children at a time. But, for this first childless week, Ruby and I busied ourselves unpacking masses and masses of school supplies. There were games and books, modelling materials and building sets; and sheets of cartridge paper, lined paper, squared paper, graph paper, sugar paper, and brown paper... There were felt-tip pens galore, socking great tins of powder-colour paint, giant paint brushes, and enough wax crayons to keep a candle-making monastery in business till the Second Coming. There was, in fact, everything: from sports equipment to sanitary towels; from shiny geometry sets to the most unyielding toilet paper I've ever come across; from the contents of the Medical and First Aid cupboards to the school's Punishment Book. This was a book in which the head teacher was to record any canings or beatings – who had been punished, the reason for punishment, and how many strokes had been administered. There was such a book at the public school I went to in the Fifties, and I am still upset by the memory of something the Headmaster wrote in it well over fifty years ago. One Head of House had beaten about a dozen boys in one session, giving them three strokes each. The Headmaster wrote in the margin of the book: "If corporal punishment is to be worth its salt I consider four strokes to be the minimum. Six is always to be preferred". Not surprisingly, he was a deeply unhappy man.

Not until 1981 was corporal punishment abolished in Inner London schools. In other parts of England, the practice was still legal in state schools until 1986, and in private schools until 1999. It was a hideous business, and there are many alive today who still bear the emotional scars caused by it.

At new Riverside, I learned that I was to spend six hours a day banged up with my group, with only two twenty-minute breaks each day – a couple of which would be lost each week when on playground duty. Each teacher had his or her own group, and we had to be with them all day, every day. This would apparently provide the continuity said to be vital to the development of maladjusted children. The sad truth is that so many of the vital things that we so often take for granted (security, meals, warmth, appreciation and recognition) were unknown to most maladjusted children.

Throughout the last weekend before the children arrived, I bit my nails and slept badly, and my bowels went into perpetual motion. On the way to school that September Monday morning, I had two fantasies. In the first, I heroically and brilliantly talked a young hoodlum into releasing the teachers that he'd taken hostage, into handing me his flick-knife, and into returning to his study of *The Iliad* under my kind but strict tutelage. In the second fantasy, I walked into the classroom and was immediately felled by a blow to the head with one of the ILEA's brand new plastic chairs.

I arrived much too early, long before anyone else, and drank cup after cup of instant coffee. I couldn't relax enough to sit down, but ceaselessly walked in and out of the classroom, in and out of the loo, in and out of the front entrance to the school. Eventually, Miriam and Steve arrived. Ruby arrived. The school bus arrived, fifteen minutes late. The adults formed a small welcoming committee at the school entrance as the bus drew up. First off was Madge, the big, beaming, blonde bus attendant. From the way they greeted each other, it was clear that she and Ruby knew each other already. Everyone knew someone in this game, except me. Madge was followed, not by the bunch of hoodlums I had been expecting, but by four small children who looked as sick as I felt, and as tired and aged and worn.

There was seven-year-old Micky, a wanderer, who at the age of four had successfully stowed away on a train from London to Bournemouth, where he believed his missing dad would miraculously appear before him. He had spent the day on the beach until he came to the attention of the authorities who shepherded him back to London. Micky was by turns falsely cheery or genuinely sullen, and was sadly unattractive in both modes. He was reputedly uncooperative, stubborn and disruptive. There was Duggie, who was ten years old - undersized, underachieving, unhappy, and also disruptive. They followed Ruby into Class 1. And there were Terry and Tom, who raced ahead of me into Class 2, where they prowled around, breaking things.

"Let's sit down and get to know each other," I said.

Terry scowled. "Why?" he said.

They were both eleven years old. Terry was an athletically built lad with fair hair and the biggest bags under the eyes I'd ever seen. On the outside he was cocky; on the inside he was a mass of anxiety. He rubbished the work I gave him. It was all too easy, too babyish - though I knew from his papers that he was almost illiterate. He wanted to spend his day roaming round the school, to see what everybody else was doing, inwardly convinced that something awful must be about to happen somewhere.

Tom was different. Tom had a chalk white complexion (after one of the hottest summers on record), a marionette-ish way of moving, and a permanent worried frown. Tom didn't roam. Indeed, wherever I sat, Tom immediately sat next to me, linked his arm through mine, gazed up at my face, and tremulously bleated: 'Do you love me?' It was a tricky question. To say 'no' (though true) seemed callous. To say 'yes' might invite an inappropriate response - anything from a demand for money to the accusation that I had made a homosexual advance. After he'd repeated the question at least twenty times that first day something inside me gave way, and I said 'yes'. Terry snorted contemptuously and began to tie bits of Meccano into knots. But Tom was delighted.

"And will you love me forever?" he said.

I tried to turn the conversation on to educational lines.

"Well, now, Tom," I said, "do you know how long forever is?"

But Tom wasn't interested in the Elasticity of Time, or the Concept of Infinity, or Einstein's Theory of Relativity. Nor was he interested in Meccano, finger painting or Sticklebrix, reading, writing or arithmetic. All he was interested in was finding out if I was going to love him forever. It didn't seem a fair question on a first date.

The school didn't yet have a playground - the builders were still working on that - so playtime was spent wandering round the rubble with Tom and Terry. Tom and I were still linked arm-in-arm, as though we were walking out together in some mad Victorian romance, while Terry loped around us in circles, hurling clods of earth into the sky, kicking half bricks at me, trying to lift any manhole cover we came across so that he could persuade or force Tom to climb down into the drainage system. It seemed that Terry was inspecting his new surroundings rather as animals do. I didn't find it a restful playtime, and then the three of us went back to the classroom for another awful hour and a quarter until it was dinner time.

Teachers and pupils all dined together in the octagonal hall-cum-gym. As we sat down at one big table, Ruby smiled and asked how it was going. I tried to smile back, but I think the strain of the morning was showing. The food was the best I had ever had at any school: beef cobbler, with mashed potatoes and greens, followed by jam roly-poly and custard. I would have enjoyed the meal hugely under other circumstances, but what I was most conscious of was Tom's vice-like grip on my fork-arm, which made it difficult to eat nicely.

The afternoon could best be described as a missed opportunity, educationally speaking. Somehow we never got down to work. Terry wanted to know all about the empty rooms further along the zigzag corridor. I explained that they would gradually fill as other children were admitted to the school, at which a shadow passed over Tom's face and his frown deepened; I think he had hoped for a more intimate life. Terry shrugged his shoulders and said that the other kids had better not be like this 'spassy-mongy', indicating Tom. Tom shot me a look of terror. I knew how he felt.

At the end of the day, I saw them to the school bus. Mercifully, Tom let go of me so I didn't have to ride home with him. Ruby and I, with Miriam and Steve, gathered in the staffroom. This became a daily practice, a chance to de-brief, to let off steam, to bandage wounds. On that first day, I lied about how well I'd managed, but I think Ruby saw through my deceit.

I went home and spent the evening not listening to my partner Sue's brilliant analysis of the methodology of her essay on Durkheim's Theory of Something or Other, but planning the next 32 years of my life - up to retirement age.

2

I had run away from Beulah Park School because running away has always been my default setting in life. It's my survival instinct, wired deep into my limited repertoire of behaviour patterns. Others among them include submitting to bullies, lying if it helps me escape persecution or even justice, and miming when I don't know the words. When I was a child, I wanted to run away from school many times, and with hindsight that seems a perfectly reasonable idea. School is the only workplace where punishment is part of the daily routine. Why would anyone want to stay in a place where they hit you with sticks and straps? But it is taking me far longer to come to grips with my non-instinctive behaviour. Intellectual understanding and learning has always taken ages – not only did I never learn the subjunctive passive perfect of *moneo*, I never understood why that verb needed a subjunctive passive perfect. I still can't imagine any situation in which I would want to say 'I might have been advised...'

Another of my tendencies is to be secretive, which is a passive form of running away. In childhood, I was secretive about how frightened I was at school because to spill the beans wouldn't have been fair to my parents, who were at pains to tell me that they were making financial sacrifices in sending me to private schools. They assured me that I was lucky not to go to a Council School as the children in such places were 'common'. This was a word applied to all those not fit to be true members of society. To be common was to be impolite, sloppy, insensitive and generally brutish. 'Common' boys didn't open doors for ladies, or raise their caps politely, or wait their turn nicely. I can remember the morning when I was in bed with mumps, and my mother came into my room to tell me that my father was fed up with me and my brother being repeatedly unable to go to school through illness, and was threatening to send my older brother to the local council school if this stream of ailments (whooping cough, measles, colds and flu) continued.

My father was prone to be exasperated by Life's Cruel Turns, some of which I was covertly responsible for. There were mornings when I heard my father calling out to God from the bathroom because his razor blade was lacerating his face. I lay in bed, knowing that it was my fault, because I had used the blade to sharpen my pencil the previous day. When my father emerged from the bathroom with several tufts of cotton wool on his cheeks and chin, I never confessed to what I'd done. Secrecy was a place of comfort that I never wished to leave.

I was born into a middle-class, south-west suburban London family just eight weeks before Neville Chamberlain flew to Munich to appease Hitler. I had a good war, most of it on a tricycle in the garden of a farmhouse in Cheshire. Sometime after D-Day we moved to the City of Bath and I went to my first school, run by Miss Wills and Miss Fuller, two sweet and kind ladies. Here, I cried for the first hour of my formal education, but perked up a bit when Miss Wills told us the story of Caractacus being led in chains before the Emperor Claudius, and held up a book with a colour picture of that memorable moment. She and Miss Fuller may well have been lovers. What I liked about them was that they never hit anyone.

My next school was Cuddington Croft Preparatory School, Cheam. It was run by nasty Mr Springman, who was nuts and hit us all. He was a man plagued by recurrent flashes of Christian belief. When the Faith was strong within him, he looked madder than usual and summoned groups of small boys to what he called The Spinney – a tiny grove of small trees in the grounds of the school. Here he conducted what were meant to be indoctrination classes, though incoherence blunted the proselytising sword. As a Catholic I was excused attending these classes, but lay meetings at The Spinney were compulsory for all.

I remember two in particular. One concerned the impending cricket match against Melbourne Lodge School. At the time, I was Captain of Cricket (though later sacked from the post and replaced by Hadaway II), and the entire Eleven was called to The Spinney for a pre-match pep talk. News had just come through that Treagus had chicken pox and would be away from school for a couple of weeks, so a replacement had to be chosen. Mr Springman told us that in his opinion the replacement should be Ridler I. He asked what I thought.

I agreed with him; to do otherwise would have been pointless and dangerous. "Yes, sir," I said. "He's a very good fielder." Ridler was useless as a batsman or bowler.

Springman glowered at me and pulled a large grey handkerchief from his pocket. He began waving it around, a sure sign of agitation. "I'm not interested in whether he can field or not, Sonny" – he called us all 'Sonny'. "I'm interested in whether or not he's a good Christian."

There was madness in his eyes, and I said nothing.

The subject of the second Spinney meeting that I remember took place in 1949, shortly after Mr Springman returned from a year's sabbatical in a loony bin. During his absence, the school was run by the Second Master, a lovely man named Bob Wright. The year without Springman had been joyful. Not a soul was caned that year and not one meeting was held in The Spinney. But when Springman reappeared, allegedly cured, meetings were immediately resumed and the subject of the first one was Leadership or, more accurately, Mr Wright's Lack of Leadership.

Springman said he hoped we all knew that Mr Wright had been only a private in the army during the Second World War. "A private! Suppose everyone in the army had been a private! What good would an Army of Privates have been?"

It was one of those moments in childhood when you discover something very important about yourself, about your political, moral and philosophical DNA. My immediate thought was that an Army of Privates would have been a sight more useful than an Army of Generals, but once again I said nothing.

I have strong and clear memories of Cuddington Croft – of the dramas enacted there and the cast of players. There was Wharfe the Handyman, who mowed the cricket ground, assembled the goal posts, marked out the athletics tracks for Sports Day, replaced light bulbs, did a thousand things and yet managed to spend most of his days in his shed, which was intoxicatingly scented with the smell of warm glue. There was the exciting winter morning when Mr Pearce stood too close to the gas fire and set fire to his gown, and the exciting afternoon when Mrs O'Keefe suddenly disappeared in the middle of a Nature lesson. It was a warm summer's day in 1949. Through the classroom's open windows we could hear the hum of bees. We were copying into our Nature Notebooks a diagram Mrs O'Keefe had drawn on the blackboard showing the parts of a flower. She was sitting on the window ledge. I remember glancing up just at the moment she crossed her legs, lost her balance, and fell backwards through one of the open windows into the hedge outside. We took no notice of her little cry, for we were obedient little boys, and simply continued copying and colouring-in our pistils and stamens.

And there was the day Mr Springman denounced Mr Gryffyd in Prayers.

We started each day with Prayers, an umbrella term for a Prayer, a Hymn or two, School Notices (announcements), and Fear. It was held in the annexe behind the main building, a bungalow that housed three classrooms and the staff room. The folding doors between Form IIIA and IIIB were opened up to create a room big enough to hold the whole school – some 110 boys, seven teachers and Mr Springman. The masters and mistresses lined opposite walls the length of the room. The boys stood in rows at right angles to the teachers, facing Mr Springman. Mr Wright or Mr Ranger (whose breath always smelt of baked beans) sat at the old upright piano. The Head Boy (the saintly Hadaway II who was Springman's favourite and had replaced me as Captain of Cricket), the two School Prefects and what were called the Senior Sixther (of whom I was one) stood separately from the others, between the piano and Springman. The Prefects and Senior Sixthers were Springman's henchmen, with the power to impose the punishment of 25 lines.

Whenever we had a cricket or soccer or rugger match against another school, parents of those involved would come to watch. The small crowd usually consisted of mothers only on weekday matches but mothers and fathers on Saturdays. At Prayers on the morning after a school match, Mr Springman always included a brief post mortem – praising Bellfield's batting or Banfill's bowling or anything that Hadaway had done, and giving anyone who had played badly a thorough ticking off. But on the morning after a match against The Priory School (we lost by 12 runs), Mr Springman went further. After verbally lashing Dell for dropping a sitter, he turned on Mr Gryffyd.

Out came the handkerchief. "And I thought the way Mr Gryffyd behaved in front of the mothers yesterday afternoon was disgraceful. "

All heads turned towards Mr Gryffyd. He took a pace forward and looked up the room at Mr Springman. "Well," he said, "I didn't think your behaviour was anything to write home about."

All heads turned to Mr Springman. The handkerchief waved furiously, but not in surrender. "See me in my study," he said.

All heads turned back to Mr Gryffyd. We wondered if he was going to get the cane. I write 'we' because I believe that every pupil at Cuddington Croft thought alike. We were cloned prep-school boys (with the possible exception of Lunt), eager to think and act as one so that by the time we were in IIIA we were almost indistinguishable, one from another, which may be why the wrong person was punished from time to time. I don't think Mr Gryffyd got the cane that day, though Mr Springman's relations with his staff were often strained. I remember the day when I was sent to the staffroom with a message for him, and arrived just in time to hear Major Kennedy assertively saying that he wanted his salary that day and he wanted it "in cash this time".

There were no such charming moments at my next school - Epsom College - where everyone over the age of eighteen appeared to have a licence to hit everyone under the age of eighteen, and all under the patronage of soft-core Christianity. We had a Chapel and a Chaplain, daily prayers, Grace in Latin before each meal, and studied, though as far as I know didn't practise, Divinity. Even our sex education was provided by a visiting Canon, an elderly man with a benign expression and a weak voice. As the sex education session was held in Big School, a hall large enough to accommodate the entire school, and as the College possessed no microphone, it was impossible to catch most of what he was saying, though we were all on the edge of our seats. The Canon's weak voice was matched by the weakness of the bulb in the slide projector so that it was difficult to make out what he was presumably describing. The session ended with a brief description of the procreativity of a young couple. First there was a slide of a young man in RAF uniform and a woman in a Utility dress. The Canon then whispered some words and, hey presto, the next watery slide was a picture of a baby – *mirabile dictu*!

As well as the usual subjects, Epsom offered – in the words of the brochure – Greek or German, Music, and Art. Greek, being useless, was for A stream pupils only; German, being the language of a still recently defeated nation was for the others. Music and Art were 'Extras' which meant they had to be paid for separately. A free but compulsory Extra was the study of warfare. Like all public schools and many grammar schools at the time, Epsom had a Combined Cadet Force. One afternoon a week and one day a year, we played soldiers. This was taken so seriously that at the age of 16 we had to take military examinations known as Certificate A, Parts I and II.

On Certificate A examination day, a party of Guards officers from Caterham and NCOs from the East Surrey Regiment arrived to put us through our paces. We had to march and show off our rifle drill, display how well we could crawl through mud and do the monkey run across tarmac, and that we knew all about Section in Attack and Section in Defence – the word 'retreat' was never used.

One June afternoon in 1954, a group of us stood on the College lawns while a thoroughly bored young Lieutenant examined us on Section in Defence. "Now," he said, "you're advancing along here... and you suddenly come under fire from... there." He pointed with his swagger stick to where the ground rose towards the Sanatorium. "What d'you do? "

None of us said 'flee' or 'scream' or 'wet myself', but as one we chorused "Dig in, sir."

"Yerrrs," he said, languidly. "And what are you going to do with the earth you dig up?"

A hand went up.

"Yerrrs? You," he said.

"Sir, we'd pile it up in front of us so that it formed a defensive barrier, sir." That was Smallshaw, who subsequently joined the Rhodesian Police Force.

The Lieutenant sighed. "No, no, no," he said. "That would give the enemy a clear indication of your position. Within a ver' short time he'd have you bracketed with artillery fire and then you'd be wiped out."

We weren't worried about being wiped out. What concerned us was pleasing this real soldier. Another hand went up.

"Yerrrs?"

"Sir, I'd spread it all around so that it was flat and didn't give away our position, sir!" That was Gower. I've no idea what happened to him.

"No, no, no, no, no, no! Abs'lutely fatal. An enemy reconnaissance plane would spot that from a mile up and you'd be bombed to smithereens. Come on! Come on! Think!"

There was a silence. We had exhausted our knowledge of Section in Defence. The Lieutenant sighed again and pointed once more with his stick – I got the impression he liked doing that. "You'd put it in that building there."

"But, sir," said a shocked voice, "that's the Chapel."

3

By going straight from school to university, where I had to repeat a year because they'd asked the wrong questions in second year exam papers, I avoided National Service, something that I have subsequently regretted. Just a couple of days ago, my brother described his own National Service days in the RAF as 'the most liberating experience' of his life. I'm convinced it would have torn me from my middle class home with its narrow horizons and its premium on behaving nicely. Instead I went to university, where my father persuaded me to study Law, although I didn't want to be a lawyer. I wanted to teach, because teachers had long holidays and that would enable me to write and paint. It never occurred to me that lawyers have even longer holidays. Not surprisingly, my teaching career began in a private school.

This was Preston House, a pre-preparatory school in the Weald of Kent. When I started there, straight from university, I was regarded as a qualified teacher although I had no teaching qualifications. In those days you could get a job as a teacher in any school in the land if you could speak your name and stand up straight at the same time; admittedly, it helped if you were a university graduate, whatever your degree. Present trends in educational policy suggest that we have returned to such madness.

The owner and Headmaster of Preston House was disappointed that my degree was in Law, because that meant he couldn't put BA after my name on the school's brochure. The initials placed after his name were FRGS (Fellow of the

Royal Geographical Society - a title granted to anyone who'd paid to be an ordinary member of the RGS for five years), so I didn't see what he was complaining about.

I had been accepted as a teacher at this strange school simply because I was vouched for by a woman who acted as a kind of nanny to one of the pupils there, a little boy whose great-great-great-grandfather had been Prime Minister back in the 1900s. The nanny and I met only once. She was smilingly nervous, and I was smarmily polite. It was, therefore, a perfect meeting, and her vouching was enough to get me the job. There was no formal interview; the Head wanted to discuss the historical novel he was writing, of which he had a high opinion, rather than education, which I think he saw as simply a matter of reading aloud to children. Then we went for a walk round the grounds during which we agreed a verbal contract of my employment. I was to receive £35 a month and my keep.

It was not an unhappy existence. The pupils were very young (4 to 11) and so well behaved that I discovered I had wasted my time in buying and reading a book called *How to Be a Successful Teacher*. In the chapter on Class Discipline, the author stressed that 'one must start as one means to go on', so a new teacher must make it clear that 'any nonsense' will not be tolerated. On my first morning, I delivered a stern address to a small gaggle of eight-year-olds, promising that, if they behaved, all would be well, but if they didn't, they would feel my wrath. All this ranting was totally unnecessary; these children had obedience wired into their DNA from way back.

Like Cuddington Croft, Preston House provided several outstanding memories. One was being given a starting pistol by the Headmaster, and told to supervise the next race. I didn't know that the dangerous part of a starting pistol is not the end of the muzzle, but the top of the muzzle, where there is a little hole out of which the hot gas escapes. I didn't hold the pistol high in the air, but on a level just a little above my ear. When I pulled the trigger, there was the sound of a bang, which I had expected, and the smell of singed hair, which I hadn't. Another outstanding memory was being stung by a wasp while I supervised the boarders as they watched *Coronation Street* one evening. The most vivid was of sitting on the bed in my little room in the Teachers Annexe one Sunday afternoon, trying to master the art of fitting a condom on my willie because marriage was looming and, in the parlance of the time, I'd never 'done it'.

As a teenager I had been deeply impressed by the writings of George Orwell, and had formed the opinion that Britain was an unjust and unfair place, and that private education was partly responsible for this, a view shared by my fiancée. So, when we were married in the depths of the appalling winter of 1962-1963, neither she nor I was happy to live in a bungalow in the grounds of the school. Six months later, despite all my attempts to achieve Mastery of the Condom, my wife was pregnant and my political conscience at last got the better of me. I resigned from the school, which meant also moving out of the bungalow and finding somewhere else to live. My wife wanted us to move to Epsom, where her parents lived, which was understandable but unwise, for her relationship with her parents was not good.

We moved in the autumn of 1963. It was perhaps a well-timed move. Preston House had only a year or two left before financial difficulties hit the school and, according to one Friends Reunited website, the Headmaster 'did a runner'. There is another, darker Friends website that suggests that his hasty departure was also prompted by revelations that he had been abusing boys. There was apparently a flurry of paedophile activity in and around Sevenoaks at the time, and mention is made of one headmaster blowing his brains out before the police got to him. No one knows what happened to the Head of Preston House. I know he had a revolver, a relic of his days as a young officer in Malaya at the end of the Second World War, because he showed it to me. It was a good job he didn't let me have it as a starting pistol.

I handed in my notice to Preston House in the autumn half term and went straight to Surrey County Council's Divisional Education Office in Epsom to seek a job.

"Well, dear," said the kind lady in the office. She shuffled some papers. "What about teaching in a school for the Educationally Sub-Normal?"

I said I didn't have any special qualifications.

"I don't think that matters, dear," she said. "And there's more money attached."

I thought it did matter, and so, instead, she made an appointment for me to see the Head of what she referred to as the Dilston Road School, Leatherhead. The Head and I met in his office. He asked me if I had ever taught girls. I said I hadn't.

He took a puff on his pipe and said: "They're different from boys."

A bit more information would have helped, but I suppose it was a start.

And so, my descent through the social classes began, for after all those years of being threatened with being sent to a Council School by my parents, I now entered one for the first time in my life. I was, at last, a teacher, for at Preston House I had been a 'master', a strange title that has no related transitive verb – you can't say 'I master History' or 'he mastered me Geography'.

My rookie year at Leatherhead was grim. The school was divided into three streams: the Grammar stream, heading for GCEs and CSEs (forerunners of GCSEs); the Technical stream, heading for City and Guilds exams; and the Secondary Modern stream, heading for miserable employment in low paid jobs if they were lucky. I taught English and Maths to a mixture of classes, the toughest of which was 3.7, the bottom stream of 13 year olds. They ran rings round me. The boys jeered at me and fought each other. The girls knitted and chattered to each other. Together, they induced in me a feeling of chronic impotence each time I stood before them, hoarsely trying to shout them down so that I could preach the Glories of Decimals Multiplication or the Wonders of English Literature. The only time I was able to deliver some sort of ordered lesson was when Danny, the Class Gang-Master, informed me at the start that I'd have no trouble that afternoon because he'd had 'a quiet word with them'. I should have made a permanent deal with Danny there and then, because he was right - I had no trouble that afternoon.

Much of the time, I was the only one in the room going through the motions of education. Occasionally, other teachers (notably the Senior Master) peered through the small pane of glass in my classroom door, their faces twisted in disapproval of what was going on. But, as the terms went by, I began to enjoy the lessons with 3.7. Each year I became better at teaching them, and each year I came to respect them more. To the rest of the staff they were 'the Remedials'. To the rest of the pupils, they were 'the Dimmos'. To me, they seemed brave and cheerful in the face of adversity, with no more bad habits or bad traits than any of us.

I stayed six years at Leatherhead, slowly developing some sort of practical teaching skill, and studying in the evenings to gain teaching qualifications through Wolsey Hall correspondence courses - which came module by module through the post on bright green folio-size paper. Most of my teaching time was still spent with the Remedials, but as a reward for the stout work I was putting in there, I was later timetabled to teach A-level History to the Sixth Form. By late 1969, all was working surprisingly smoothly. At which point, I felt it was time to move on professionally. I also wanted to run away from a marriage that was becoming increasingly unhappy for all involved. True to form, I thought it best to do this secretly. I slunk off, drove to a rented flat in an unfashionable part of Greenwich, and moved my bank account from the Epsom High Street branch to the one at Waterloo Station - poised, as it were, to flee the country via the Boat Train.

I then turned my back on friends and relations, and started a new life, applying simultaneously for a teaching post with the Inner London Education Authority (known as ILEA), and for a place on what was called their TOSLADIC course (for Teachers of Slow-Learning and Difficult Children). It was the last wise career move I was to make.

The TOSLADIC course was run by Mary Evans, who was not only an ILEA Inspector for Special Education but also the ex-Head of a couple of schools for what were then called 'maladjusted children' - in those days you labelled the child, not the condition. All teachers love being on courses - it's like playtime to them - and there was a lot of fun on Mary's course. We spent two days a week being lectured by theorists and instructed by practitioners. For the other three days, some of us were placed in a variety of special schools (for the Deaf, the Physically Handicapped, the Maladjusted, etc.), some in mainstream junior schools in tough areas, and some in special units in secondary schools. I went to a junior school in Brixton run by a large and fierce man who swiped at the children as they scuttled past him along the corridors. On my first visit, he took me to a classroom from which a lot of noise was coming. He flung open the door and all the noise stopped instantly, save for the sobbing of the middle-aged, deeply depressed teacher who was bent over her desk with her arms wrapped round her head.

"Maybe not the best moment to call," said the Head, clearly unimpressed by her misery. "We'll come back, Miss Cook, when you're feeling better." But she never was.

By far the most valuable components of the Course were the sessions with Mary Evans. Apart from Denis Barnham, Head of Art at Epsom College, Mary was the first person I came across in any form of education, whether as pupil or teacher, who was inspiring. She was passionate about the need for special schools to provide not only education but also relief, understanding and comfort for deeply damaged children. I realised that teaching those who were often regarded as the dregs of the educational system was work every bit as important and as subtle as teaching gifted children. It was a priceless lesson and one that society forgets at its peril. It's a disgrace that we have forgotten it repeatedly in the last thirty or forty years.

The ILEA Course finished in March 1970, and the following month I started teaching at Beulah Park, a Boys' Comprehensive in Wandsworth. It was a nasty school, housed in a Gothic pile that had been in turn a Victorian orphanage, a First World War clearing hospital for wounded soldiers, and a Second World War prison camp for captured SS officers. It was run by a sextet of cane-mad desperadoes (the Head, the Deputy Head, and the four Housemasters – one of whom, clearly a Charles Dickens fan, threatened to cut children in half with his cane), who openly acknowledged their contempt for the very children who most needed a sympathetic regime, the children that Mary had championed on her course, the children I wanted to teach.

The job I had applied for was Deputy Head of the Remedial Department. I was interviewed by the Head of the Lower School and my immediate superior, a gloomy man named Winters. There were three other candidates for the post. When we had all been interviewed, there was half an hour's wait, and then I was called back in.

"We'd like to offer you the post," said the Head of the Lower School.

"Thank you," I said, and then there was an awkward pause until he asked if I was going to accept the post. Ever obedient, I automatically said 'yes', and the moment I said that, I thought: 'Shit! I don't want this job. I shall be miserable here.' But the fatal word of acceptance was out of my mouth and the deed was done - I believe a surprising number of people go through the same emotions at the altar when they say 'I do'. It took me less than a week to discover that I hated the place, but well over a year to do anything about it.

Matters came to a head one Friday afternoon in May 1971. I was going through the intricacies of decimal coinage with First Year Delta (*delta*, for goodness sake! What was this? Plato's Academy?), and I had managed to get them quiet after poor but repulsive little Barnes had finished his *petit mal*, when chairs and desks started raining down from the classroom above on to the gravel path outside our windows. The floor above was reputedly haunted, and I wondered if ectoplasm was at work.

"What on earth's going on upstairs?" I said, as another desk crashed to the ground.

Barnes looked at his watch. "Oh," he said, "that'll be French Conversation."

One of the few things I am proud of having done at the school was to support a twelve-year-old remedial lad who had been summoned before both the Head and Deputy Head on a charge of gross impudence or something... I forget what. The boy was rattled by the Gestapo-like interrogation to which he was subjected. He kept saying 'No, I never done nothing', and the Deputy Head repeatedly pounced on this and said: 'Ah, then you must have done *something*!' And then the boy repeated 'No, I never done nothing', and the Deputy Head said 'If you didn't do nothing then you must have done something', and the thing kept going round and round in circles. I tried to intervene, but neither the Head nor the Deputy Head was interested in what I had to say. I think the Deputy Head wanted to provoke the boy into losing his temper, because then they could cane him, which was what they wanted to do. I knew that if it came to that, I would have to step in physically and, if necessary, try to wrestle the cane from their grasp. In the end, they let him go, and the Head then turned to me.

"You didn't approve of that, did you?" he said.

I told him I didn't. It was the moment when we both knew that we would have to part.

While my professional life was in transit, my private life was in tatters. When I moved to Greenwich, it was to live with Sue, a student at Goldsmith's College and a former A-level pupil at Leatherhead. Even now I have difficulty in working out exactly what I thought I was doing, but I suppose Sue gave me the chance, at the age of 31, to have the adolescent romance that I had totally missed out on in the 1950s.

Once it became known that we were not married, Sue and I were evicted from the flat in Greenwich, and went to live with Linda and Phil, two friends of Sue, in a vast late-Victorian house in Brockley. The house had been empty for many years, had fallen into decay, and needed restoration. Linda and Phil were very slowly rebuilding it, and converting it into four flats. Sue and I lived precariously on the first floor, which was really the first joists, for the woodworm-riddled floorboards had been ripped out and burnt in the back garden. We had some electricity from lead-sheathed wires, some gas seeping from rusty cast-iron pipes, but no hot water. I boiled a kettle to shave in the mornings, and used the showers at school to keep myself socially acceptable.

The passion between Sue and me soon passed its high-water mark. She had discovered that she was in love with a very nice bloke who was one of my fellow teachers at Beulah Park. In what I then considered a gentlemanly act (like raising my cap or holding a door open), but now see as me being stupid, I chauffeured her to the colleague's flat so that she could inform him of his good luck and her warm feelings for him. Disappointingly for Sue, he turned out to be gay. I drove her home in tears (hers, not mine), and I think our love never really recovered from that strange night.

At the time, teachers were not well paid, and I was poor. I know that middle-class people tend to exaggerate what passes for poverty in their lives ('… we had absolutely no money for a proper holiday, so we got an absurdly cheap flight to Rhodes and practically lived off bread and cheese and olives and sardines and the local wine…'), but three-quarters of my salary went in maintenance to my wife and children, and I had to sell most of my belongings - mainly LPs and books. I held on to my trombone, madly thinking it would lead to fortune. I was playing in three bands: the Goldsmith's Big Band; a jazz-funk ensemble called Battalion, led by Colin Towns; and Ken Hyder's avant-garde jazz group, Talisker. The hope was that, one day, Talisker or Battalion would hit the jackpot and all my financial worries would disappear. But for now, Talisker played in dark London jazz clubs, and Battalion made excursions to the USAF bases in East Anglia and the West Midlands. The takings at these gigs just about covered travel expenses. Some days I had to walk to and from work, a distance of roughly eight kilometres, and most days I joined the queue of screws from Wandsworth Prison at the local baker's to buy a lunch of 10p's worth of bread pudding.

A week after my dash to see Mary at County Hall, I handed in my notice at Beulah Park. The Head appeared almost as relieved as I was, though for a different reason. I thought I was OK but his school was shit; he saw it the other way round. I had only been there for three and a bit terms, but I had clearly made my mark as regards not fitting in. As far as I remember, there was no leaving present.

4

Planning the next 32 years of my life was one thing, living it was another. Everything in the World of the Maladjusted was new and strange and baffling, and that included my first Psychiatric Meeting, held at the end of my second day at New Riverside. This was to be a weekly gathering of the teachers, the psychiatric team, and the childcare staff from the hostel attached to the school. Miriam had told us very little about the childcare staff. As yet, the hostel had no children, but eventually, it would be home for up to 20 children from Monday mornings to Friday afternoons. The idea was that this would give respite to those parents who were finding life with their own maladjusted child a strain, and would also provide extended care and treatment for the children. To bring cohesion to the two institutions, Miriam was not only Head of the School, but also Warden of the Hostel. It was a pity, therefore, that she didn't rate childcare very highly as a profession.

At the meeting, it wasn't hard to distinguish the psychiatric team from the hostel staff. The former looked mature, jolly and confident; the latter looked inexperienced, sad and apprehensive. This was understandable for, with one noble exception, the psychiatric team would have little direct contact with the children, while the hostel staff would be living with them. Senior among them was the Deputy Warden, a quiet man, but with a sardonic and tough underbelly. The Domestic Bursar proved to be the best organised adult of all of us at New Riverside. She made lists, and she dealt with every item on them, in good time and in the right order.

Throughout the meeting, the rest of the hostel staff remained largely silent. I adopted an attitude towards them similar to that of a veteran of Mons meeting members of Kitchener's New Army.

Psychiatric teams in all ILEA maladjusted schools came in packs of four. The leader of our quartet was the Consultant Psychiatrist. Dr Knottingham-Forrest had an air of superiority, which seemed appropriate, as an air of inferiority ill becomes any sort of consultant, least of all a psychiatric one. I didn't immediately (or subsequently) take to her, no doubt because of some transference or projection or repression or massive Oedipal Complex on my part. I said very little at the meeting, fearing that lack of familiarity with the work of Freud, Jung, Adler, Klein, and Frohm might at any moment mean Goodnight Vienna for me.

Our Educational Psychologist – Ed Psych in the vernacular - was Mrs Lumley. She was refined Scots, with pursed lips and a serious manner and long rayon drawers, though you only noticed the drawers when she crossed her legs in meetings. Most of the time I could understand what she said, which disposed me to like her, though I hadn't the slightest idea what she did. Diana Cavendish, our Psychiatric Social Worker, was aristocratically posh, with a voice that echoed the female leads in British movies of the 1940s and 1950s. As Diana's job was to visit the families of New Riverside children Ruby and I wondered how she'd fare in darkest Deptford or on the Peckham estates. But, in truth, Diana did what I think she might have called 'frightfully well'.

The last and most charismatic member of the psychiatric team was our psychotherapist, Arthur Barron. I did have some vague idea as to what a psychotherapist was supposed to do, and it rapidly became clear that Steve and Miriam looked to Barron for insight and firm guidance. He had been deeply involved in the selection of children for New Riverside, several of whom were already his patients. I thought I detected friction between him and our Consultant Psychiatrist, and by the end of the afternoon I knew who I wanted to win.

The meeting lasted two and a half hours, during which time I developed an acute headache which I hoped indicated I was learning something.

Desperately seeking aid, advice, a role model, and the possibility of sex sometime in the future, I seized on Ruby's suggestion that we occasionally combine our dynamic duos, so that there was a chance of one adult slipping in some teaching while the other acted as law enforcement officer. In doing so, we discovered that, besides Everlasting Love, Tom was interested in 1001 Useless Things to do with Raffia, New Horizons with Finger Paint, and Mrs Brinn's Dressing-Up Box. Ruby had a chest of unwanted clothes from the Inner London Education Authority's Costume Department - a nice line in doublets and hose, Jacobean jerkins and rakish Regency pantaloons. But Tom's favourite outfit was a floral, cretonne frock, and each morning he would dash from the school bus into Ruby's room, throwing the contents of the tea chest all over the place until he found... the dress.

"Aha!" he would cry, in a cracked soprano voice, for the more excited Tom became, the higher his voice was pitched. And he would pull the frock over his sweater and trousers, and enter another world. It was always an interesting spectacle, though getting him back into the real world afterwards took a bit of doing.

Whether transvestism fitted in with the psycho-dynamic approach, I wasn't sure. Miriam had said that we weren't to encourage disturbed behaviour, but at the same time we were not to shrink from dealing with it as it emerged. She said, very firmly: "The children are here because they're disturbed and that's what we've got to help them with." Then she usually added, in a voice which contained a bit of a sneer: "Anyone can teach them to read."

Certainly, the floral cretonne frock brought out Tom's disturbance beautifully. By the middle of the second week, he had barely time to zip himself into it and shove a cushion up the front, before rushing from Ruby's room, shrieking that he was pregnant. He habitually made a bee-line for the school gates, ran into the road and lay down, giving the inhabitants of the estate a running commentary on the progress of his labour. Ruby and Lil Barnes, the school attendant, usually reached him just as he shrieked: "Oh, my God! The waters have burst!" They helped him up and led him back into school, while I tried to stop Terry pelting him with builders' rubbish. It was so easy to be sucked into the drama that I only just stopped myself telling Terry that I didn't think that was the way to treat a woman on the verge of motherhood.

After only three days, psycho-dynamism had exhausted me, and I shifted over to Behaviour Modification. In so doing, I discovered that both Tom and Terry responded eagerly to reward points – a sort of home-made system of Green Shield stamps. By dinner time both of them had filled pages and pages of their exercise books with sums - every one of them wrong. When I tried to show them how to get their sums right, Terry was furious because I was stopping him doing more sums and earning more points. Tom wasn't angry, but Terry's anger frightened him and he begged me to let Terry do more useless sums before something awful happened. Behaviour Modification madness was maintained throughout dinner, where they both earned extra points for not throwing mashed potato at Micky's sullen face - even though he was asking for it – and for the whole afternoon reward points were maintained as Terry and Tom slogged on. At the end of the day, when the bus arrived to take them home, they were beaming with satisfaction at a job well done.

Though they had learnt absolutely nothing, I was tempted to keep the points system going the next day, for the sake of peace and quiet. I argued with my conscience that this process was going to help the three of us bond together, but my conscience told me not to be an arsehole. It was Friday, the last day of the school's second week, and time for another Craft Lesson. I wanted to hold back the raffia, for emergencies. And then I had a brainwave. Back in 1970, one of the components of the course run by Mary Evans had been a workshop session on *How to Develop and Print Your Own Photographs*. That was what we would do. It couldn't fail. I was on a winner.

Terry, Tom and I wandered round the school, taking photographs of Ruby's group (I grabbed any opportunity to visit her classroom), of the Hostel, of the builders, and of the insides of people's nostrils. Then, after dinner, the three of us went into the walk-in stock cupboard of our classroom, to develop and print the film. Though large, it didn't really have enough space for three to work together in comfort. And we weren't exactly working *together*.

Once we were settled in the cupboard, I told Tom and Terry that I was going to turn off the light so that it was safe to take the film out of the camera. I stressed that once I had turned off the light, they were not to turn it on again until I said they could. I turned off the light. Tom, anxious to make sure he knew what light he was not to turn on, said: "What light? This one?" and turned it on. I shouted to him to turn it off, which he did. But then Terry gave a silly laugh and said: "What harm can turning the light on do?" and turned the light on again. I turned the light off, and the three of us somehow bumped together in the dark. I heard Tom say "Blimey", and then somebody threw a punch – I have no idea who, but I know it landed on my chest. As I rubbed that better, I tried to instruct Terry in how to take the film out of the camera and wind it into the developing tank. Then I heard the sound of Tom climbing up the cupboard shelves, like an animal seeking safety in height. I told him to come down, but he didn't. There was a loud 'Clunk' and the air filled with choking powder.

In panic, I turned on the light. Terry shouted: "Turn the fucking light off! " I apologised and turned the light off, but not before I had seen what was making us all cough. Tom had knocked down some large tins of powder paint. The lids had come off and we were in danger of being suffocated by a mixture of chrome yellow and burnt sienna. I repeated my order to Tom to come down, but he said it was too dark to see, so I switched the light on again, at which Terry ordered me to: "Turn the light off, you fucking cunt!" I did as I was told, but insisted that Tom was to climb down, which he did, bringing with him books, pens, pencils, craft knives and more tins of powder paint.

It was only then that I heard the noise of laughter coming from outside the cupboard. I opened the door and fell out of the cupboard, followed by Terry and Tom. All three of us were covered in paint. I blinked in the light and wiped some of the powder from my eyes. Ruby and Lil Barnes were sitting on one of the classroom tables. They had brought Duggie and Micky into my classroom to witness the fun. They had been listening to what must have sounded like the dialogue and sound effects of a badly-tuned Radio 4 play. After the children left on the school bus, I cleaned myself up and limped to the staffroom where Ruby was in hysterics recounting the afternoon to Steve and Miriam.

And so ended my first fortnight as a maladjusted teacher, two weeks in which I felt I had aged rather than become experienced. I had a great need of alcohol, and a strong desire to go and live high in the Welsh mountains and deal with old sheep. I couldn't believe how inept I was at looking after just *two* 11-year-olds. I racked my brains to identify what the problem was, apart from my complete inadequacy.

It seemed to me that the basic flaw in the work I prepared for Terry and Tom and, indeed, in everything I offered them, was that it was too complicated for Tom and too babyish for Terry - or so Terry said - though I already knew that Terry was no smarter educationally than Tom. Terry turned up his nose at whatever I placed before him. He pretended to be insulted when asked to read a bit from *The Green Pirate*, kicking open the door and walking out of the room. Tom at least showed enough interest to ask why the pirate was green. I explained to him that, like Captain Kidd the Queasy, The Green Pirate was notoriously seasick for much of his buccaneering life, and learnt in the process that, if you have to explain a joke, it simply isn't funny.

Though I couldn't believe the weekend would give me time to recuperate, I found I was looking forward to Monday and returning to New Riverside. Thinking about this, I discovered that what I was really looking forward to was seeing Ruby again.

5

The first two girls arrived in late September. According to expert opinion, maladjusted girls were extra-dynamic, so I made an effort to appear totally in control when they arrived. This was ruined by Tom giving birth to his tenth phantom child and by his endless demands that I love him forever, as well as Terry's repeated demands that I fuck off. It wasn't the start I'd hoped for.

The newcomers were Sally and Anita. Sally was six years old, tiny, with long copper ringlets. She looked the embodiment of Dickens's Little Nell, but came to us with a reputation that would have made Bill Sikes shit himself. She had lasted less than a week in the Reception Class of her Infants School before most of the parents had threatened to withdraw their traumatised offspring, and her teacher was on the point of resignation. Sally lived with her mum and two younger sisters; one of whom, Sally explained proudly on her first day, "makes bubbles wiv her bum in the barf". The entire family needed help every bit as much as Sally, and at a later stage we seriously considered inviting her mum and sisters to move into the hostel. Being very young, Sally went to Ruby's group, where she was so unctuously welcomed by Micky that some of us felt sick.

Anita was eight years old, square-shouldered, lively, and carried the usual health-warning of being disruptive. She lived in a children's home called Temple Beeches, way outside the catchment area for the school bus, so arrived at New Riverside by minicab each morning. Temple Beeches was a combination of independent village and closed community set in acres of scuffed grass and empty flowerbeds. Anita still received occasional letters and visits from her dad, but had lost all contact with her mum. Terry and Tom, who had got used to each other in the two weeks they'd been at New Riverside, gave her a frosty welcome. Maybe they reckoned there weren't enough Green Shield stamps to be shared among three.

At the sight of Anita, post-natal depression descended on Tom. He sat beside me, clamping my arm with one hand and pointing at Anita with the other. "Why's she here?" he said, in what I think was supposed to be a whisper.

"'Cos she's fucking mad," said Terry. "Like you."

I wondered if I should protest, but soon realised that Anita was tough enough to stand up for herself. She watched rather than participated for the first part of the morning, but sprang to life when Lil Barnes came in with the milk. Lil, with her tiny husband and her seven children, lived on the estate, up the road from the school. Everyone loved Lil, the embodiment of what the child in all of us craved. She gave out the milk, mended the children's battle-torn clothes, bathed and plastered all our wounds, and handled our tantrums. She took care of the staffroom, made us tea and coffee, brought us biscuits, made us laugh, and never said anything about the children that I didn't understand. It was Sally who applied the most appropriate label to Lil when, in a moment of tiny rage, she screamed at us one afternoon that we were all pigs, then turned to Lil and said: "An' you're the muvver pig!"

Lil's room was just round the corner from the little lobby that led to Ruby's room and my room. Each classroom had an electric buzzer connected to a display panel in Lil's room. If ever we needed rescuing, all we had to do was press the buzzer. Lil would see which room had called her, and hasten to our aid. That was the plan. In practice, the children pressed the buzzer so often that the system went into overdrive and then meltdown on the very first day, and was never reconnected.

As the days stumbled by, I learned that I needn't have worried about Tom and Terry's attitude to Anita, which passed from initial resentment and a challenge to her right to be with us, to reluctant acceptance, and finally a seldom-voiced but genuine concern for her. This was a pattern often repeated. With some children the concern went deep, with others it was shallow rooted, but nonetheless it was there.

In early October, the builders at last completed the playground. It was roughly 30 metres long and 12 metres wide - about the size of a large swimming pool - edged with 3-metre-high chain-link fencing, and smoothly surfaced in shiny new asphalt. Its primary intended use, we were told, was as a five-a-side football pitch. In the sixteen years that I was at New Riverside it was used as a great many things - cricket pitch, sports stadium, parade ground, studio lot for an ambitious crime video, and artillery post from which to pelt passers-by with unripe pears from our own trees.

Tom had other uses for it. At a pinch it could be the labour ward, though he still preferred the middle of the road for that. It could also be the stage on which he lost himself and entered a wild world of his own. At playtime one morning, he found a broken umbrella on the grass that surrounded the playground - presumably lobbed there by a local resident. Tom picked it up, and examined it, frowning and blinking with a 'what-have-we-got-here' expression reminiscent of Tigger having his first mouthful of Eeyore's thistles. Then he started strutting up and down, swinging the umbrella in Burlington Bertie style. I don't think he knew what an umbrella was. He took it for a walk round the playground and then suddenly violently attacked it, hurling it into the air, stamping on it, pulling its ribs out one by one, like God did with Adam.

"It's a seagull!" Tom shouted. "Blimey!! Fucker-bugger!!!"

With the removal of each rib, Tom's voice rose, and his knees leapt into the air, as though he was a member of the Royal Marines Drill Squad auditioning for the Royal Ballet. Eventually, his screams of "fucker-bugger!" reached Miriam's room. She, too, had a loud voice.

"Tom!" she snarled.

Immediately, Tom came to rest. His knees fell. His voice descended three octaves. He dropped what was left of the umbrella. He blinked rapidly, and passed a trembling hand upwards over his forehead.

"Fucker-bugger," he gasped, and strode stiff-legged from the playground.

Tom, Terry, Anita and I jogged on for a couple of weeks, and then ten-year-old Marianne arrived. She had a loud, husky, grown-up voice, and smelt dreadfully of urine (she was a chronic bed-wetter - as I had been at her age). She made it clear from her first day that she wasn't going to put up with any nonsense. When Terry tried to make her feel unwelcome, she rasped at him that he could shut his fucking mouth. And he did. The exchange sent Tom into one of his blinking attacks and made him move his chair so close to mine that he was practically sitting on my lap.

"Blimey," he said, and he stared up at my face, hoping to find comfort and reassurance in my eyes. I felt sorry to let him down so badly.

Marianne brought two innovations to Group 2 - we didn't have 'Classes' at New Riverside, but simply named each group after the number of the room it occupied; so my children and I were Group 2, Ruby and her children were Group 1. The first innovation was song. Marianne loved to sing. Her early favourite was a variation on an old Music Hall song:

> *Daisy, Daisy, the Coppers are after you.*
> *If they catch you, they'll give you a month or two*
> *They'll tie you up with wire*
> *Inside a Black Maria*
> *So ring your bell and tiddle like hell*
> *On your bicycle made for two.*

When I tried to persuade her that it wasn't 'tiddle' but 'pedal', she would have none of it. It was the first of our many clash-of-wills, the vast majority of which she won hands down. So we all joined in and sang her words.

Her second innovation was to bring a New Order to New Riverside. On her second afternoon, she decided that we should play 'schools'. I had hoped that some of us at least were trying to do that for real, but her pretend version was far more confidently directed than mine, though it may have set the psycho-dynamic approach back a year or two as far as Tom was concerned.

Marianne always came to school dressed in the remnants of her old school uniform, an indication perhaps that she believed in the old methods. Certainly she awoke old memories of old fears and old failures in all of us. In her pretend school, she cast herself as 'Miss White', the teacher. Although we'd only known her a couple of days, I don't think any of us was surprised that she had selected the lead for herself in our little psycho-drama, but her choice of name contained an element of surprise. Marianne was a mixed race child, and I wondered whether 'Miss White' was an odd or significant name for her to have chosen. Either way, Marianne's interpretation of that role made us gasp. Miss

White - in the voice of a corncrake – placed us at separate tables, and ordered us to sit up straight. She then outlined the school rules. There was to be no talking at any time - except lots from her. We were all to do our work. If we looked up from our work, we would be caned. If we dropped anything, we would have to stand in the corner for three hours. I tried to negotiate this down to two (actually, I would have accepted two and a half), but there was nothing doing. If we got our sums wrong, we would have to do them again - twice. The list went on and on, each rule punctuated by the occasional "Blimey" or "Fucker-bugger" from Tom.

I tentatively put up my hand to ask what would happen to anyone who refused to join in, but Miss White threatened to send for my mother. Since my parents had taken such a dim view of my recent divorce, I did as Miss White said.

Heads down, we began the work that she ordered me to supply. And that, of course, was her big mistake. Once we'd done the sums, poor Miss White hadn't a clue whether our answers were right or wrong. Marianne sidled up to me, trying to be charming. She asked me to mark the sums for her. But by now I was thoroughly into my *role* as pupil, and delighted to have relinquished my *job* as teacher. Not caring if I got caned, I pointed out that she could hardly expect me to mark the other pupils' work.

Miss White moved to a level of intended charm that must have hurt. "Oh, please, Yakky," she begged, using the name that I had been given by the children. "Please!" It was my first moment of power since I'd arrived at New Riverside.

I was learning a lot, every day, and that afternoon was an eye-opener for me. What these children needed, above all else, was a sympathetic regime and as many 'second chances' as it took to make them feel secure. But what they *said* they wanted, what they demanded, was a rigid and unforgiving structure, a regime so punitive it would stop them going wrong. The school they mistakenly craved was one where cruelty would force them to conform, and where, at the same time, the deprivation they suffered would reinforce their belief that everyone hated them because they were so bad. What they didn't want to hear - at first - was any suggestion that they could bring about change, that there were solutions to their problems, and that they were going to have to make tough decisions for the future.

The silly thing was that the strict discipline that they claimed would stop them being bad had so far been totally useless. The moment they came up against unbending authority, they rebelled, and kicked and spat and fought until they were ultimately thrown out of the school or the cinema or the park or wherever. At first, they didn't want anything to do with the alternative approach that we offered, because it seemed to hint that there was something wrong with them, which they construed as saying they were 'mad'. It was immeasurably better, as far as they were concerned, to be 'bad' than 'mad'. So their initial response to the invitation to talk about something that had gone wrong (why there had been a punch-up at playtime, why they'd torn up their best piece of work, why they had taken a craft knife to the school football, when football was what they most enjoyed), was to shy away.

They were adept at this, employing a variety of techniques. The simplest, but least successful, was to deny that they'd done whatever it was that they were accused of. 'Oh, yeah? Can you prove it? Was it me?... Was I though?... Who says?... Did you see me?...' And when we said 'Yes, we did see you', they would demand photographic evidence (hopeless for me – I'd given up photography). This technique seldom worked because they usually made sure that we or somebody *did* see them. They wanted to be caught. This was where hope lay. This was the first step toward something being done that might stop them erring again in the future.

Slightly more successful from their point of view, and certainly more provocative from our point of view, was the 'So what?' attitude, an acceptance of the deed, but a denial that it mattered, shrugging off the guilt and challenging to our ability to do anything about it. This was often accompanied by the vehement assertion that they'd been 'all right' at their other school; it was 'this fucking dump' that was the problem. When we asked why they had been kicked out of their previous school if everything there had been all right, they shouted back that it was because one of the teachers there 'had it in for me'. This teacher would invariably be labelled illegitimate.

The third technique was to hurl responsibility back at us - 'Why didn't you stop me then?' This was also the question that educational administrators sometimes asked when presented with the monthly bill for window repairs. But at least it was an indication that they wanted to be stopped. Life for them was an endless quest to find some place where their dreadful behaviour would be contained. They came to New Riverside hoping that, for a few years, we might be that place. After New Riverside - well, there was the Army (never the Navy or the RAF), prison or the police force - these last two being seen as interchangeable.

In discussions about life after school, we argued that they were the only people who could put a brake on their wildness. It wasn't outside control they needed, but interior control, self-control. And to gain self-control, they had first to gain self-esteem, which in turn meant understanding and acceptance of self. All this we explained to them, many, many times, at different intellectual levels, in a variety of ways.

And they all replied: 'So what are you lot gonna do about it?' But almost without exception, they eventually joined in the dialogue, the process. And then we were struck over and over again by their courage and resilience, and by the flickering glow of that tiny spark of hope that they had somehow kept alive within them.

By mid-October my group numbered five: Tom and Terry, Anita and Marianne, and Daryl, a duplicitous lad who always looked as though he was searching for a suitable place to plant a bomb. I still spent much of most days racing about like a demented cowboy, trying to round up my Group and get them back in the corral. I had long given up Green Shield stamps, and had turned to open bribery. I offered sweets, biscuits, even sherbet dabs in return for co-operation.

In desperation, I turned to money. One afternoon I thought I might be on a winner when I announced a Silence Competition, with 5p to whoever could keep his or her mouth shut the longest (5p could buy an immense amount of sherbet in those days). I had to explain this several times to Tom who, once he had grasped it, said he thought it was very kind of me. Marianne's eyes flashed - she never had any money - and she immediately clamped her lips together. The Silence Competition began. But it didn't work. I hadn't thought it through. The moment one of them spoke they knew they were out of the competition, and therefore had nothing more to lose by going on speaking. And now there was a lot they wanted to say about what they'd do to the lucky fucking bastard who eventually won the competition and pocketed the fucking 5p. To get them back on board I kept having to restart the competition, and then those that hadn't previously spoken were loud in their protests that it wasn't right that the noisy loud-mouth bastards were getting a second, or fourth, or (in Marianne's case) tenth chance. And as soon as they said that, the noisy bastards shouted 'Who's fucking talking now?', and we all started arguing about the rules of the Silence Competition.

So I let Miss White take over for the rest of the afternoon, and we all sat at separate tables and were frightened into silence. I think we were all a little afraid of Marianne. She could conjure up an air of authority that I envied, and she was so quick to establish her authority. One dinner time, when there was pineapple upside-down cake for pudding - a much prized treat - it was Anita's turn to serve the second helpings. Anita cut what was left into six pieces, one for each of us. But it wasn't an easy job to make them all equal in size, and one piece ended up noticeably bigger than the others. As soon as she'd finished cutting, Anita served the first and biggest bit to Marianne.

Daryl narrowed his eyes, and complained: "Marianne's got the biggest bit."

"So what?" said Marianne.

"The reason you get the biggest bit is because Anita's scared of you," said Daryl, who was also scared of Marianne.

"No, it's not. It's because it's 'ladies first', you fucking pig!" snapped Marianne, and Debrett couldn't have phrased it better.

A few days later, the first weekly boarders arrived at the hostel. The following morning they swaggered out, crossed the little driveway between hostel and school, and made their entrance. Jimmy, Simon, Larry and Mike were all teenagers and they were all to be in Steve's group - Group 5. They followed Steve up the corridor to Room 5, at the far end of the school. Simon and Larry wore DMs; Mike wore shoddy trainers; Jimmy wore what looked like running shoes without the spikes. Simon had tattoos. Jimmy had a foxy expression and light fingers. Mike was sadly overweight. Larry had a slouch hat, which he was loath to take off. At morning break, the four of them emerged from their classroom, swaggering with false bravado as they ostentatiously fingered their cigarette packets and boxes of matches, until they were sharply told by Miriam that there'd be none of that.

Though pocket-sized, Miriam had tremendous authority. The children obeyed her, and so did the adults, even the school-keeper. Always hoping to discover some magic means of establishing my authority over children, I watched Miriam closely to see whence came this ability to make people do what she wanted them to do. Was it the power and force of her personality? Was it her frightening demeanour? Was it something to do with her being a woman? Or was it simply because she was Head? After all, she was respectfully addressed as 'Miss Daniels', and Steve as 'Foster', while Ruby and I were referred to as 'Brinnie' and 'Yakky' respectively. Was it because Steve was tall, and cool in manner, with an air about him that suggested he had considerable experience of just about everything going on, whereas I was giving the impression that I had never before seen anything that was anything like anything that happened at New Riverside.

Predictably, the arrival of the big boys resulted in Ruby's children and my children giving in, without any sort of struggle, to the temptation of repeatedly rushing up the corridor to see what was going on in Steve's room. For much of the time the corridor was a little like Lewisham High Street on a Saturday afternoon, with Steve's mob stomping down to our end to find out what was going on and wreck it, and members of Ruby's group and mine darting up to Steve's room to reciprocate.

Marianne was my worst offender. Even unprovoked, she paid Steve's group several visits a day, throwing open the door to Room 5, leaning against the frame, smiling seductively and projecting what was meant to be irresistible charm until Simon or Jimmy or Larry, or all three of them, told her to fuck off. Mike never entered into any of this. Like my Tom, he was an obsessively teacher-centred child, more interested in delivering monologues than trading punches. After she had been told a sufficient number of times to 'fuck off', Marianne returned to my room in a smouldering bad mood. Acting out of a rare spirit of sisterly solidarity, Anita would then sprint up to Room 5, shove her head round the door and tell Simon and Jimmy and Larry and Mike and Steve to fuck off, and then sprint back to me.

Always happy to have a reason to come pillaging down our end, Simon and Jimmy and Larry would then set off in pursuit of Anita. When they crashed into my room, Anita leapt behind me, giggling and yelling at me to save her. Sometimes a few blows were struck, most of which landed on me as I interposed my body between the invaders and the invaded. All I could do was remonstrate with both, after which Simon, Jimmy and Larry moved on into Ruby's room to sneer at the 'baby' things that Duggie, Micky and Sally were doing. This sneering process took progressively longer, and those sneering increasingly lingered in Ruby's room. In the end, Steve - with poor overweight Mike padding behind him - had to come down the corridor and shepherd Simon, Jimmy and Larry away from the sand-and-water tray, with which they loved to play, and take them back where they belonged.

But Terry was still my habitually worst wanderer. He repeatedly told me that he wanted to be in Steve's group, which he clearly saw as a considerable educational promotion, and a chance to learn to read by some kind of osmosis. For him, as for many others, membership of Steve's group was a status symbol. This was a common syndrome at New Riverside, the belief that the granting of status would automatically and almost overnight bring with it skills and abilities they never had before. With status, there would be no need for graft or hard work. Terry had the wild hope that if he was in Steve's group, he'd be instantly be blessed with the essential skills that had so far eluded him in six years of schooling. This was a commonly held belief, which exacerbated the wandering problem.

At the next psychiatric meeting, we discussed 'the Phenomenon of Wandering'. Bunny Barron explained that when children ran away from the room they were supposed to be in, they were hoping that the adult looking after them would set off in pursuit, away from the other children. Thus, the wanderer wouldn't have to share the adult with the other children. The solution to the problem was for us adults to stay put with the children who were being good and not wandering. This would force the wanderers to give up and return to the fold. At the meeting it was unanimously resolved that the adults would in future stay put when children went a-wandering. I was hugely comforted by Barron's explanation, and relieved. From now on, I would know what to do.

The next day, Ruby, Steve and I spent most of the time sitting alone in our respective classrooms while all the children roamed wildly round the school. Except Tom.

6

I have no recollection of being involved in drawing-up the School Timetable at New Riverside. It must have taken place during that blissful first week BC (Before Children) when I was happily checking out the school's facilities and stuffing my walk-in cupboard with supplies – including the tins of bloody powder paint. But I don't think my mind ever connected specialist materials with specialist subjects that would have to be timetabled. In all my years as a teacher, timetables have never been my thing. Down in Room 2, we didn't need a timetable; we just had double periods of 'Practical Anarchy'. But every teacher knows, that whatever appears to be happening in a classroom, there has to be a piece of paper somewhere that says it's really Maths or History or Business Studies.

On our pieces of paper, it said that the first work session lasted from 09.15 to 10.45. Group teachers had complete freedom as to how to divide that time, and even as to when we took our morning break. The idea behind this was that, when the pressure reached bursting point inside the classroom, we could release the safety valve by going out into the playground. This free-wheeling system didn't last long. Once Steve's group was up and running it meant that there was nearly always one group or another taking time out and thereby disrupting the groups who hadn't previously reached bursting point but were now seething with rage because others were having playtime. So we ditched that system and switched to a set playtime for all groups from 10.30 to 10.45.

Each morning, I intended the first period to be reserved for the essentials of education, the meaty stuff. If I had any say in the matter, our day would start with Mathematics, then move on to Reading and Comprehension, and finish with a kind of educational *digestif* - references to important events in the news; or a group discussion on the Meaning of Life; or perhaps, if we were in frivolous mood, a quiz. In any event, the first session ended at 10.25 with the arrival of Lil Barnes carrying a crate of small bottles of milk.

In reality, the arrival of the milk was the only part of the first session that ever ran according to plan. Wherever they were, whatever they were doing, the clink of milk bottles was enough to bring my group to heel. The sound even carried like a tocsin to those who were outside the school grounds, in the Woodland Walk that ran behind the school, or in the Labour Ward on the street.

At 10.30 it was officially time for play, which meant that, perversely, several of my group then claimed they wanted to stay in the classroom and do 'work'. The children seldom used the word 'learn' or 'learning'. They saw Maths and Reading and History and every other subject simply as a task they had to perform, a bit like Tom Sawyer having to creosote the fence, or slaves picking cotton, or like some of the less high-concept projects of Roosevelt's New Deal. No academic advance was ever expected. There was no such thing as progress, development, improvement. In their eyes, such an aspiration as 'learning' was never part of the contract. They would 'do work' in the manner of rock-breaking gangs on Dartmoor. In a way, work was their gift to me. It was all they could manage, because their minds were seething with worries - about home, families, friends (or lack of friends), failure, bullies, murderers, disease and illness, madness, violence, rivals, rows, revenge, sex, strangers and siblings (born, unborn, and as yet un-conceived). Learning to read and write seemed to them not only nigh on impossible but also totally irrelevant, given the appalling state of their world.

Playtime usually dragged on because, as in every school in the world, teachers not on duty did not hurry to leave the staffroom. But, even when I wasn't on duty, I soon gave up the idea of going to the staff room. Twenty minutes seemed so little time, and I had this feeling that it was better to keep your face in the shit, rather than lift it out, only to have to put it back in so soon afterwards. So, if I wasn't on patrol, I usually joined in the impromptu football in the playground. Captains were appointed ('Why's he captain?... He's always fucking captain... I've never been captain...'). Teams were picked ('Why pick him?... He's fucking useless... You never pick me... I'm not fucking playing...'). We kicked off. And there was surprisingly little foul play, except for the time when Daryl the Bomber deliberately tripped me on the edge of the penalty area, and I fell and dislocated my little finger. I stood there, staring at it and wondering if it belonged to me, until Steve walked briskly over, told me to shut my eyes, yanked the finger out of joint, and then let it snap back into its proper place.

At the end of playtime, there were no bells or buzzers summoning children to Assembly. Teachers appeared at their classroom windows, signs were made, and most of the children came in to the Hall. Those that didn't were not pursued, unless they were very angry, very upset, likely to do much damage or hurt themselves or run off. If all they wanted was to climb on the roof and hurl insults through the skylights at the rest of us, we simply ignored them, remembering Barron's words that we mustn't let the wayward have us all to themselves.

The basic idea of Assembly was that we should sit in a circle of chairs, the circle expanding as the number of adults and children in the school increased. We put the chairs out, helped by those children who were either anxious or happy to lend a hand. The rest watched critically from the wall-bars. One of the difficulties in gauging how a maladjusted child feels, is that you can never know to what extent presented behaviour is a true indication of their emotional state. Maladjusted children may dance on the roof because they are having a shit time, or because they have caught the mood of some of their peers. They are unlikely to be dancing with joy; that's not how they show relief from worry and sadness. In like fashion, though they might sometimes help to put out the chairs because they felt in a generous mood, it might just as well be because one of their mates has ordered them to, or because they'd just done something awful and felt they'd better try to bank a little goodwill before this came to light.

So there we would be, round about 11.00, sitting in our circle, ignoring the clog-dancing on the roof and the obscene gestures being made at the windows by the non-conformists outside. There was no formal entrance by the Head; Miriam had usually joined the rest of us to put out the chairs. There were no fanfares. There were no Bible readings and no hymns. In the early 1970s, schools were required by law to set aside a part of each day for an act of corporate worship, and most schools complied by including a bit of Christianity in their assemblies. But there were many that didn't; it depended on who among the staff were the more pushy - the believers or the non-believers. At New Riverside, Steve, Ruby and I were fervent disbelievers, and Miriam was alone in her Faith. She was the child of Jewish parents, but had rejected Judaism in her late teenage to convert to Christianity (after which her parents had held a funeral service for her). She wanted at least an element of worship in our assemblies.

That wasn't easy. Worship works best in an atmosphere of calm reverence. When Miriam said, "Now, let's put our hands together, close our eyes and say a prayer..." she was asking too much of most of us. Our children needed to feel impossibly secure to close their eyes in a public place. The concept of religious worship did not come naturally to them, and they believed that adopting an attitude of prayer was asking to have the piss taken. It seemed to them (as it did and still does to me) weird. I don't think you can reasonably expect children, whose lives have been a succession of strange, frightening or destructive events, or indeed of those whose agony arose not from external events but from inner turmoil, to put their faith in an all-powerful extra-terrestrial force who reputedly loves us all. The philosophy of the school was much more solidly based in suggesting that we put our faith in psycho-therapy, in counselling, in talking problems through, in seeking to gain insight. And to do that didn't require worshipping graven images of Karl or Sigmund, or the lighting of candles, or genuflecting, or the burning of incense - all of which could have been deliberately misapplied. For a while Miriam tried to keep the concept of Prayer for the Day going, but reason prevailed and she gave up.

Our assemblies were simple affairs. News was delivered. If any child or adult was absent from school that day, we were told why they weren't at school, for the children did not take what amounted to disappearance lightly. In their short lives, many of them had already experienced the sudden loss of parents, siblings, nans and grand-dads, and other key figures. Even if they professed to hate the absentee, they had to be reassured that he or she hadn't come to any harm. Similarly, notice was given of any expected visitors, so that the children knew who visitors were and why they'd come. Strangers were distrusted. In the children's experience, strangers were often the bearers of bad news, and sometimes dangerous.

Local news followed, which encompassed anything of note that one of the groups had done, was doing, or was about to do: school outings; the 'showing' of something someone had made or painted or grown; rarely, the reading of a story someone had written. Then came a kind of post mortem on events of the twenty-four hours since the last Assembly. This had nothing to do with misdeeds in the classroom (which should have been dealt with there and then), but were more in the nature of crimes against the school as a whole, a bit like the work of the International Court of Justice at The Hague. If there was nothing serious to report (like arson of Her Majesty's Dockyards, or Sedition, or Dirty Work with a Wax Crayon), then there was more time for singing.

To my eternal shame, I once shopped little Sally during one of these post-mortems. I had been on duty that playtime, and while patrolling the school in an easterly direction (arm-in-arm with my fellow Community Officer, CPC Tom) I had come across Sally sitting quietly by herself at a table in the Library, cutting up books with a pair of blunt scissors. She seemed very happy, but the look on CPC Tom's face confirmed my suspicions that what Sally was doing was wrong. When I made my report at Assembly, Miriam was outraged.

"Well, I'm certainly not going to have people in my school cutting up my books…" She went on and on, lashing Sally with her tongue.

Sally was superb. With all eyes on her, she sat through Miriam's tirade, beetroot red with embarrassment. When Miriam finally paused to draw breath, Sally hit back. She was good with words. One morning, Maureen was proudly showing her Moonstone ring to the older girls. Sally had somehow joined this group and Maureen asked her what she thought of the ring.

"It's like snot," said Sally.

So here, in Assembly, Sally leapt in.

"Tain't your fuckin' books. Tain't your fuckin' school. It's our books and our fuckin' school."

Miriam's mouth fell open, but she graciously accepted the truth of what Sally had said. It was hard not to cheer.

When Assembly ended, we all went back to our classrooms for the second work session of the day (in my dreams), from 11.15 to 12.30, when it was time for dinner. School dinners were cooked in the school kitchen by Mrs Dixon and her helpers, and served in the Hall. There was one table for the junior section of the school (Ruby's group and mine), and one for Steve's mob. The food was good and there was lots of it. It seemed that the Special Education Department at County Hall understood the enormous importance of good food to maladjusted children. Waste is a terrible thing, but when you are feeding distressed children there has to be more than enough, so that each child can rise from the table without feeling they need to eat more. Failure to supply that little bit extra will most likely result in more waste, because the children will usually reject what they regard as inadequate, so an entire meal might be wasted. Our children needed lots of good food, and they appreciated it.

After dinner, the children went out to play or fight while Lil and the teacher on duty patrolled the school grounds to check that none of the manhole covers was missing, that there were no new gaps in the chain-link perimeter fence, and that the drainpipes were still attached to the walls. The other adults nipped into the staffroom for yet more coffee and a quick fag. If the children wanted to smoke, they had no choice but to go the toilets (not very pleasant) or round the back (far too obvious). In fact, it didn't really matter where the pupil-smokers went as they were always shopped by their mates. After a very short time, smoking ceased to be a problem. Even the smallest of the children realised there was little need to swagger and show off, and therefore less reason for smoking.

Playtime ended at 13.15 (according to the timetable) and was followed by Work Session 3, which lasted from 13.15 to 15.00, without a break. As far as I was concerned, the afternoons stretched before me like those last eleven miles to One Ton Depot must have done to Scott of the Antarctic. We used the afternoons in a variety of ways. Steve did proper woodwork with his lads in the Art and Craft Room, so proper that they all came thundering down the corridor at the end of the afternoon proudly brandishing the dove-tails, rebates and mitres that they had made. Ruby's group often worked with sand and water. I put my faith in Plasticine, paint, and balsa wood (called 'blazer wood' by the children, whose instinctive approach to cutting any shape out of a virgin piece of the wood was to start in the very centre of a large sheet, thus maximising the wastage). What I liked about blazer wood was that nobody got hurt when they were clobbered with a piece. One afternoon a week we went swimming: Steve's group on Monday, Ruby's group and mine on Friday. Tuesday and Thursday afternoons were for Games, which meant football in proper kit in the autumn and winter, and cricket in any old gear in the spring and summer, both played down on the ILEA playing fields, some ten minutes' walk away.

The children went home or back to the Hostel at 15.00. We tidied our classrooms (mine was always, absolutely bloody *always*, a complete shambles by the end of the day), and staggered to the staffroom for tea or coffee and increasingly lengthy de-briefs on events of the day. On Fridays, some of us dashed to the Bank to get cash for the weekend before it closed at 15.30, and then back to New Riverside for more coffee and more de-briefing. It helped enormously to talk together about where things had gone wrong, and why, and what could be done to make them not go wrong another time. As that first year wore on, it helped even more when some of us augmented Friday afternoon's coffee with a slug of brandy.

7

New Riverside was the first of the ILEA's purpose-built school-and-hostels for maladjusted children, a new concept in education for the Authority. Consequently, the blind were leading the blind, for none of us working there had any experience of such a place. Not only that, only Miriam among us had been on the staff of any sort of maladjusted school. She had taught at Meadowbank, an older step-sibling to New Riverside, just a stone's throw (or whatever else came to hand) from King's College Hospital. Miriam was not forthcoming about her experiences there, though she often began sentences with the phrase 'When I was at Meadowbank...' Steve had run a Tutorial Unit (a one-teacher school for a maximum of ten pupils - great if you liked autonomy, but otherwise lonely) and, after several years teaching in ILEA Infant and Junior Schools, Ruby had just finished a year at the London University Institute of Education getting an Academic Diploma in the Education of Maladjusted Children. As for me, I stood magnificently alone in having neither experience nor qualification related to what I was doing.

Back in 1969, when I applied for a place on Mary Evans' course, I had been interviewed by Dr Watson and Miss Prosser, two formidable ladies, high in the ILEA Special Education power elite. They were a sort of double act, renowned throughout County Hall. One of the questions they had asked me was 'Did I play a musical instrument?' I said I did. They wanted to know what instrument.

"The trombone."

There was something in the way they then bent their heads together that appealed to my sense of secrecy, and when Dr Watson said to Miss Prosser (out of the corner of her mouth): "Could be useful…" I wondered briefly if I was to be parachuted behind enemy lines armed with a sackbut. Instead, I was made unofficial Head of Music at New Riverside.

In one of the many corners of the school hall there was a brand new upright piano, but we had no pianist. Having appointed me Head of Music, Miriam insisted that it was time for this title to be justified. She suggested that, if I couldn't play the piano, I must learn the guitar, to provide music for assembly. I happened to have a guitar that I'd bought for a tenner in Kingston in the early days of my marriage, before I fully realised that marriage would allow no opportunity or encouragement to strum. When I left Epsom, I took the guitar with me, so now I bought a cheap How to Play the Guitar tutor, and spent a weekend in October 1971 learning the chords of G, C and D7. Once I had gained sufficient expertise to switch from one chord to another without a two-bar pause, I asked the children in each group what songs they'd like to sing.

Tom didn't know what I was talking about. Micky pouted and shrugged his little shoulders. Duggie said: "All of them." I said I didn't know that song and did he mean *All of Me*? He said 'no', he meant all the songs there were. Steve's group were more helpful. They wanted *Tom Dooley*, and Simon particularly wanted *Spirit in the Sky*, a semi-spiritual that had sold a couple of million copies in 1969 and 1970, and had reached Number 1 in the British charts.

I think Simon may have liked *Spirit in the Sky* because of the very special guitar sound achieved on the original by Cavendish Da Shiel. If you check on Wikipedia, like I did, you will find that Cavendish "played the lead guitar parts on Spirit, using a 61-62 SG Les Patrick, a 68 Marshall Plexi 100w half stack and a home-made overdrive box in front of the Marshall..." Unfortunately, I didn't have any of those things, I had only my £10 acoustic guitar and, even more unfortunately, Norman Greenbaum had written Spirit in the Sky in the key of E. My fingers were as yet incapable of playing the chords of E, A and B7, so I had to transpose the song into the key of G, a third higher, and it became a sort of Spirit in the Stratosphere. Singing it, my voice faltered and fluttered into a wobbly falsetto, and the song lost much of its heavy and insistent power. But Miriam liked it because a religious tartness attached to it, being about Jesus but written by someone Jewish, which satisfied both her past and present faiths.

On the Friday before the October half term, I gave Ruby a lift to Euston after school. We talked. I learned that she was married to a guy who taught in Manchester, and that she commuted at weekends to join him there, which was why we were headed for Euston. I told her about what I regarded as my guilty past, and she was sympathetic and understanding in a way that no one else had been - in fairness to others, I suppose that was partly because I was as secretive about my feelings as I was about everything. I dropped Ruby at Euston, and drove to Francis, Day and Hunter in the Charing Cross Road to buy the sheet music that would bring the muse to New Riverside.

After half term, a pale ray of sunshine appeared on the teaching horizon. Back in September, Mrs Askew (keen, kindly and kulinary) had been appointed as a part-time teacher of Domestic Science, with a little quiet sewing on the side. The plan was that each afternoon she would teach a different group: Ruby's on Monday, mine on Tuesday, Steve's on Wednesday. Theoretically this was to give the group teachers time to write reports, read the referral papers on children on the school waiting list, and to consult with the psychiatric team 'Who Were There To Help Us'. But the whole Domestic Science scene would rely, not only on Mrs Askew's preparedness to take my group, but also on the reciprocal preparedness of my group. Mrs Askew was due to start work on the last week of the first half term. I never joined my hands in prayer, but I did hope it would all go well.

On arrival, Mrs Askew announced her plans. The older girls (Anita and Marianne) were to make some pretty little curtains for the windows of the Home Economics room in which, over a period of time, the children would learn to make fairy cakes and biscuits. She spoke of getting them to make paper doilies; of brightening the Home Economics room with little bunches of flowers, plucked from the nearby Woodland Walk; of teaching the children how to eat cake with a fork. This last ambition was quickly dropped in place of trying to persuade Sally not to eat raw pastry with a knife. Mrs Askew was perhaps a touch over-ambitious. She hankered after daintiness and peace and stillness. My group didn't. They believed in noise and movement. They liked the way eggs splattered when they were thrown against a wall, and the way bags of flour exploded on hitting the floor. And they were interested in the collection of knives in the kitchen drawers.

Mrs Askew started with Ruby's Group one Monday afternoon. Ruby had been looking forward to time away from her Group so that she could sit in the staffroom with a fag and read the papers on some of the children who were in the pipeline to be admitted to New Riverside. But little Sally had other plans for Mrs Askew and Ruby and the Home Economics room that afternoon. Sally took with her a fistful of wax crayons, slipped them into one of Mrs Askew's brand new saucepans, popped the saucepan on the back hob of the electric cooker, switched the hob on and waited. It took a little while before the smell of melting wax hit Mrs Askew's nostrils, and much harm had been done to the crayons and the saucepan before Sally's experiment was brought to an end. When Mrs Askew remonstrated with her, Sally told her she was a 'fucking cow', and that was the end of Ruby's chance to read the papers on children to come and have her fag.

It had been decided, though not by me, that while my group was making cakes and doilies with Mrs Askew, instead of having an afternoon in the staffroom studying reports, I was to take Steve's group for Music. This would enable Miriam and Steve to spend the afternoon chatting with the psychiatric team about how well the school was progressing, and would enable me to coax Steve's lads through a repertoire that initially consisted of *Sugar* (four weeks at Number 1 for The Archies in 1969), *Raindrops Keep Falling On My Head* (Number 1 in the charts in 1970), *The Banks of the Ohio* (a 19th century ballad of love and murder, revived by Olivia Newton-John in 1970), and *Leaving on a Jet Plane* (Peter, Paul and Mary's Number 1 hit in late 1969). It would also necessitate my learning three new chords on the guitar - F, B*b* and C7 - each one fiendishly difficult.

I had the school's entire collection of musical instruments and all six of my chords ready for Mike, Simon, Larry and Jimmy as they shuffled in. They were not impressed. Simon wanted to know why there was no Fender guitar (no idea), no Marshall amplifier (no idea), and no pairs of 30-inch speakers (no idea). Mike said he had a trumpet at home that he didn't want, and that he'd be prepared to sell to the school, cheap. Jimmy sat on the window-sill, jiggling his knees and taking a tambourine to pieces. But Larry sat at the drum kit, tilted his hat back in the manner of Sinatra and said he thought this was 'all right'.

They were fed up with *Leaving on a Jet Plane* and *Spirit in the Sky*, both of which we'd overdone in Assembly, but they still liked the gloom, misery and death of *The Banks of the Ohio*, and also my solo rendition of *Tom Dooley*, demanding several encores. I kept pointing out that the idea was that they should join in. They could sing. They could hit things. There were even things they could blow down. No, they didn't want to do any of that. They wanted to sprawl on the tables and listen to me singing about the 'poor boy' who was 'gonna die'. After a while, they wanted only the last verse and chorus, the bit where death is near. I obliged, though I'm really a complete *oeuvre* man, myself. By the time Steve arrived to take them back to Room 5, there were blisters on three of the fingers of my left hand, my throat was very sore, as though I had myself been hanged, and the repeated executions had plunged me into a deep depression.

Just as Steve's group was leaving, my Group returned from Home Economics with the biscuits they had made. Steve's lads tried to grab the biscuits. There were many shouts of 'fuck off', drowning out Mrs Askew's report on how good my children had been, and how she looked forward to taking them again. A savage fight broke out over what were now biscuit crumbs, most of which were trampled into the lino.

While the fight raged, Mrs Askew attempted to tell me how especially good and helpful Marianne had been. I could imagine her sucking up to Mrs Askew, and I heard her unctuously thanking Mrs Askew and saying how much she was looking forward to cooking again next week. When Mrs Askew pointed out that there wouldn't be any cooking next week because it was half term, Marianne's manner changed abruptly. I was slowly beginning to read the signs as to what my children were really thinking and how they were feeling. As far as Marianne was concerned, the fact that she was not going to be cooking with Mrs Askew next week as good as meant that she would never be cooking with Mrs Askew again, in all possibility would never see Mrs Askew again. That had been Marianne's experience of similar occasions in the past, and she saw no reason why this would be any different. What, therefore, was the point in making any kind of emotional investment in this process? It made little difference telling Marianne that she would be cooking with Mrs Askew a fortnight later. A fortnight is a very long time for a maladjusted child.

A few days later, Steve's Group cooked and they came down to Room 2 to offer me some of the cakes they had made. It was kind of them, and I was touched. But their glee in telling my Group to keep their fuckin' hands off led to another fight, and it was an unhappy bus-load of children that drove out of the school gates at going-home time. Steve's lads, *en route* to the Hostel, stood and jeered and made wanker-gestures at the departing bus.

Over the next few weeks, our repertoire of songs steadily grew. Chuck Berry's *My Ding-a-Ling* had its Age of Glory. I liked it because it was cheery and did not dwell on separation or death; the children liked it because it was rude. Our signature tune gradually evolved as Simon and Garfunkel's *Feelin' Groovy*, which I loved because it had only three chords and was swingy. Later, we even wrote one or two of our own songs. The younger children were fond of one which celebrated a bit of garden that we cultivated at the back of the school. In what was basically a mixture of London clay and builders' rubble, we managed to grow one or two summer vegetables, and some of the hardier flowers. To celebrate our horticultural success, we wrote a song called *Please Don't 'Sturb our 'Sturtiums*. Here's Verse 2:

Please don't 'sturb our 'sturtiums,
They're not there for you to pick.
If you 'sturb our 'sturtiums,
That's simply a cowardly trick.
You may think it funny to see us dismayed
At the sight of our seed-er-lings all disarrayed,
But how would you like a faceful of spade?
Our 'sturtiums are not there for you.

But the New Riverside song that I shall remember until, like Tom Dooley and the unnamed victim on the banks of the Ohio, I shuffle off this mortal coil, is Don Black and Walter Scharf's *Ben*, written for the movie of the same name and taken to Number 1 by the very young Michael Jackson.

It hit the charts in 1972, a year after the School opened, and was Marianne's favourite. I can see her now - standing on the table, hair all over the place, clothes covered in paint and food and grime, head thrown back, and singing her heart out. And I can hear her still - her showbiz voice, a cross between Liza Minnelli and Sammy Davis Junior, giving it everything she'd got, while I desperately tried to get my fumble fingers round chords I hardly knew as I accompanied her:

Ben, you're always running here and there,
You feel you're not wanted anywhere...

And, though we did the best we could, that was exactly how she felt.

8

ILEA granted me a day's leave to move house, so I missed the last day of the first half term at New Riverside. Sue and I transferred our few belongings from the flat in Brockley to a semi-detached house in Ladywell. My father had generously given me the deposit to buy the house. It was a large late-Victorian semi, with four bedrooms and a three room cellar-cum-basement. Sue had taken the initiative when it came to choosing our new home and I had meekly nodded approval of everything she said. The children at Preston House weren't the only ones with obedience wired into their DNAs. What mattered was that the repayments on my fixed-rate Lewisham Council mortgage were only £25 a month. When moving day arrived, the elderly couple whose house it had been for decades were loath to leave, and Sue and I had to prise the old man's fingers from the door frame to get him out.

Half term was spent in a dusty and dirty welter of knocking down internal walls and pulling down false ceilings, sanding floors and slapping paint about. The orgy of physical destruction was mentally very restorative, and released much of the tension within me. I could see why children at New Riverside were so fond of breaking things.

On the Monday morning after half term, I arrived early at school. I had decided that my priority henceforth would be 'preparation, preparation, preparation'. I sat in Room 2, filling page after page of the children's exercise books with lovely work for them to do - money sums, number squares, tangrams, crossword puzzles (1 Across: Animal that rhymes with "hat" [3]), Complete the Sentence games, Find the

Missing Word games, quizzes (Name four vegetables that start with the letter 'C').

The children arrived, and my Infamous Five (Tom, Terry, Anita, Marianne and Daryl the Bomber) all raced into Room 2. They were angry with me for taking the day off on the Friday before half-term, but their anger abated when they saw all the hard work I'd done for them in their exercise books. This was more like it. If I would fill their books for them on a daily basis, work would no longer be a problem. When I pointed out that their task was to provide answers to the questions, to fill in blank spaces, to think and to write, to add and subtract, they were not so keen, but they had a go. Most of them did most of the money sums. The stumbling block was that none of them could read. I spent a long time explaining to Tom what a crossword puzzle was, then a longer time trying to explain what 'rhymes with' meant. Neither he nor I was happy with his response to 1 Across: 'An animal that rhymes with Hat' – three letters. Tom's answer was 'DGGD'. But he did brighten up when I told him the answer to 'Name four vegetables that begin with the letter C', was 'a cauliflower and three carrots'.

This prompted me to wonder if humour might be the key to academic progress. My group liked jokes but, as their appetite for telling jokes and listening to jokes grew, mine shrank. Whole mornings were passing with nothing but jokes. The main craze was for 'Doctor, Doctor' jokes and 'Waiter, Waiter' jokes: 'Doctor, Doctor, I feel like a pair of curtains', 'Oh, pull yourself together…'; 'Waiter, Waiter, do you serve stuffed crabs?', 'We serve anybody, sir. Sit down.' Tom couldn't quite grasp what the whole joke phenomenon was about, but he eventually made one all his own.

As the putative comedian, he had the first line. Whenever and wherever it occurred to him, maybe thirty times a day, off he went: "My dog's got no nose." I then had to reply: "How does he smell?" and Tom's punch-line was "Bloody awful." And because he didn't really understand even his own joke, there would be a moment's pause before he gave the phoney laugh that I disliked immensely, and then we would go through the whole appalling routine again. In desperation, I tried to teach him another joke.

After half an hour's rehearsal it was time for him to go on stage. I called the group to order. "Ladies and Gentlemen, will you please put your hands together for the one and only Tom!"

"Doctor, Doctor," he piped, "there's a fly in my soup." It didn't work. Half the audience were bemused rather than amused, and the other half told him to fuck off. It was exactly like late-night stand-up at the Edinburgh Fringe.

That Friday, Ruby and I took our groups to the local Swimming Baths for the first time. Dick the Driver drove us there in the school bus. The cubicles in the Gents' Changing Rooms afforded scant privacy, and I wasn't too sure about undressing in front of Duggie, Micky, Tom, Terry and Daryl the Bomber, but a teacher must also be a leader, so I stripped off. They stared hard as I removed my trousers and pants, and formed a little giggling queue to catch a glimpse of my willie.

Tom frowned, and blinked a lot. "Blimey," he said, but I didn't think it was in any way intended as a compliment. Micky, with his customary sickeningly matey approach to me, gave me one of his saucy smiles and said something about "what a funny little winkle". Duggie, a very mature ten-year-old, laughed coarsely.

It was time to frighten them. "I hope you all can swim," I said.

Micky's lower lip quivered.

"Swim?" said Tom, going whiter than chalk. "Why?"

"Because this is a swimming baths," I said, "not a paddling pool." It was nasty of me, but male maladjusted teachers do turn nasty when their winkles are derided.

In truth, I didn't say any of the above, because I've seldom been touchy about my willie (whatever people say), and I'm not instinctively cruel to children. But a regular, though infrequent problem at New Riverside was anger management among the adults. We were working in an environment where a lot of anger was flying around. In the 17 years that I worked in maladjusted schools, I saw teachers grab children, shake children, slam them up against the wall (not at New Riverside), drag them into school, and slap them. And I have to admit that sometimes I slapped them, and often I grabbed them and tried to restrain them. Looking back, it seems a wonder that no child ever complained to mum, dad, nan, social worker or Education Officer.

What would we have done at New Riverside under the conditions that prevail today, when physical contact with children is not permitted? We did smack children – not often, but sometimes. I think we probably shouldn't have done. And we certainly held them, to stop them hurting themselves and others. I guess we would have started from a different standpoint and, hopefully, would have kept our arms folded or our hands in our pockets. We would have established a system with a far more rigid structure as to how to deal with wild behaviour. Instead of lashing out ourselves in response, we would have imposed other sanctions - a time-out facility, perhaps more temporary exclusions, certainly a contract system, whereby children agree that they will behave themselves and parents agree that they will come to the school whenever they are needed. It would have been extremely difficult, and whatever the system it would have been swiftly stretched to near breaking point.

What we did do, was to make sure that any violent act was not seen as the end of the matter, but rather as the beginning of a long process of seeking a solution to the problem. All the adults regretted 'losing it', and most of the time we apologised to the child involved. I believe that the children recovered far more quickly from such occurrences than we did. At the end of a school day when a teacher had sparred or traded insults with a child, or had in some other way lost self-control, the rest of us did what we could to give constructive support with the aim of making it less likely that such a thing would happen again. If that wasn't enough, there was always the opportunity to consult with Barron, confidentially. But some adults could not work in a setting where so much anger existed, and understandably decided to move on to pastures new and more peaceful.

That afternoon at the Baths, I discovered that Terry and Anita were good swimmers. Duggie and Marianne swam adequately. Daryl swam slyly, as though he was looking for somewhere to stick a limpet mine. Tom and Micky and Sally were starting from scratch with one of the instructors, a jolly man with a beard.

We swam, we towelled ourselves down, we dressed, and Dick the Driver took us back to school. Dick loved these Friday outings because Madge, the school bus attendant, had captured his heart. Ruby and I weren't surprised. Madge was a showbiz style blonde, exuding huge confidence, with a wicked sense of humour, and boundless energy. Dick was thin and gangly, and very formal (he called me 'sir'). But love lent him the wings of determination, and that afternoon, after all the children had been dropped off, he asked Madge out. Hysterical with laughter, she told us all about it in the staffroom on the following Monday morning. Dick had approached the date stiff with anxiety, or in Madge's own words, with 'every bit of him stiff except the bit that matters'.

That Friday night, I looked at my willie in the mirror of the wardrobe that Sue and I had inherited from the previous owners of the house in Ladywell. It was, I think, the first time I had done such a thing since the childhood day my mother had asked me if my brother's balls had dropped. At the time, I didn't know whether they had or not. I hadn't heard anything in the bedroom that my brother and I shared that sounded like balls dropping. And, as for my own balls, I couldn't tell, because I hadn't made a note of where they were before they might have dropped. Examining my willie, standing with my legs wide apart and lowering my head as far as it would go to get the right perspective, so far that I became dizzy, I feared that Micky was right. It was a funny little winkle.

9

As a teacher, though still very much a novice when it came to maladjusted children, I was increasingly appreciating the qualities that these children possessed. In the first place, they were incredibly brave. The vast majority had somehow survived lives that were both horrible and miserable, and hadn't given up hope. In the face of adversity, disappointment, injustice and chronic ill-luck, and worse, they kept going. They picked themselves up and hurled themselves back into the fray. I was also learning some of the misleading techniques that they employed to survive. If someone they liked announced that he or she was leaving, they said 'good fucking riddance', when what they felt was the pain of loss. It had happened with one or other of their parents in many cases. It had probably also happened with a much-loved grandparent. It had happened when they were finally and permanently excluded from their previous schools. When they uttered that phrase, just for a moment, it made them think that they weren't losing anything they valued. And when the parent or teacher or school lost its temper with them, they had the distraction of a right old row to protect them from experiencing any sense of pain and loss. The same process, from a slightly different angle, was to be seen in Assembly, when they derided any work of their mates that was being praised. 'Wanker!' they shouted. 'Fucking goody-goody', though they were awash with envy, and were in all probability fond of the person at whom they were jeering.

I was also slowly coming to terms with the psychiatric team. I still didn't like our haughty and arrogant Consultant Psychiatrist, but I admired Diana, the Psychiatric Social Worker who took her job very seriously. It can't have been easy. Diana came from an aristocratic background, but was now knocking on the doors of some of the toughest housing estates in south London, never knowing what she would find when the door was opened to her. She occasional sighed when reporting such visits: "There was jam on the door knob… and on entering one's shoes stuck to the floor…" Professionally, she had descended through more social classes than I had, but she was wise and capable..

Barron was an inspiration and a hero, a man who had spent his entire life fighting for causes he believed in, whether for the International Brigade in the Spanish Civil War or on behalf of deprived and difficult children. When we discussed what we were trying to do at New Riverside, he slapped his thigh and said: "Gosh! How thrillin'!" (the 'g' was always dropped when he became excited). I still felt a complete and utter novice, but Barron had a genius for finding hope where all seemed disaster, and for identifying little things that Ruby and I had done, and building them up until we felt we had achieved near miracles. He also convinced us that one small good thing could outweigh a host of mistakes, and that, once a child had made progress, even if that child subsequently regressed, he or she would be able to recover any lost ground far more quickly than the original advance had taken.

Barron was also a true professional, keeping strict confidentiality regarding what went on in psychotherapy with the children. Tom was a regular attender. Every Tuesday morning Barron would pop his head round the classroom door, beam at us all and invite Tom to come for his session. Tom went off amiably enough, following Barron like a trusting Labrador, to return forty minutes later, high as a kite, voice like a banshee, knees bouncing up past his ears, eyes bright with madness. The worksheets on simple division that I had painstakingly prepared didn't stand a chance.

We were now into November, always the most unpleasant time in the longest and worst term of the scholastic calendar. It was dark and cold, so cold that the children seldom ran off into the open air but found new places to hide within the school, like inside the vaulting horse at the back of the Gym equipment store-cupboard. The afternoons were especially grim. A feeling of permanent exhaustion descended upon me. I tried to keep the work going in the mornings, but by two in the afternoon my expectations were not often of an educational nature, and I grabbed at anything that offered the slightest chance of keeping us all gainfully employed.

I tried Drama, but this proved to be much too volatile. Whatever story we were enacting ended in a fight - a real one. I gave up Drama after Sleeping Beauty drew blood when she punched the Handsome Prince in the mouth. I tried model-making but, with the classroom radiators full on, the fumes from the tubes of blazer wood glue made us all over-excited. I tried Art, but the cleaning ladies objected to the mess at the end of the day, and I got fed up with Tom's endless series of pictures of what he called 'plop-plops'. Here, he was ahead of his time. Concept Art was not yet in full stride, whereas today his *Plop-Plops XIV* could well be worth a fortune. Ruby, meanwhile was having great success next door with her sand-and-water tray, which still attracted Steve's group. They swaggered down, superior in manner and smelling of the fags they'd smoked in the toilets on the way down, to spend ages in Ruby's room, making rivers and pools and harbours and mountains and roads. When Steve came to reclaim them, they insisted they'd been helping Miss Brinn with 'the little ones' - the same 'little ones' they'd just been elbowing aside and calling 'fuckin' bastards'.

It was Ruby's idea occasionally to pool our children for the entire afternoon, an extension of the way we'd shared the original quartet in the very early days of the school. The professed justification for doing this was that the children all needed help in building relationships and having enriched social experiences - all of which was true. So we joined forces, and Ruby and I took our combined groups to the parade of shops, about a ten minute walk away. Ruby told me the working classes called it 'going tats', and the Posh Boy added it to his vocabulary, thereby moving another step closer to Plebdom. Going tats worked well. The promise of sweeties if they behaved worked wonders on the way to the shops, and their relief at having been good when the sweets were doled out and we were on the way back to school made us all relax.

I didn't realize that Ruby had her own motives for going tats, not dissimilar to my own. My hope was that, on such occasions, I might be able to take Ruby's hand - in a jokey sort of way, as if I was a jolly uncle sort of figure - but the opportunity never came. Tom always grabbed one of my arms and Marianne always grabbed the other. Tom tried to stop her. I think he wanted to link both his arms with mine, which would have meant walking behind me in a kind of full-nelson. Marianne asked him if he was "a fuckin' queer?" He didn't respond until we were in the crowded newsagents, buying sweets. Then he asked me in his piercing voice what a fuckin' queer was.

The early winter weeks passed. Weekends were spent working on our house. The knocking-down bits were highly therapeutic, but I was worried about the reconstruction that would have to follow. I've never been any good at plastering or cementing, or bricklaying or, as I now discovered, at cutting quarry tiles. I wanted to create a sort of hearth in the dining part of the kitchen-diner. Sue and I had knocked out a hideous fireplace and chucked away the old and failing gas fire that it housed. In so doing, we had discovered a chimney and a perfect place for an open fire. I could manage laying whole tiles; it was when I had to cut them in half, or worse, cut them into L shapes that I ended up with fistfuls of useless gravel.

Before I left school one Friday afternoon, with the brandy warm inside me, I went to Donald the Handyman for advice, for he was, by his own admission, a craftsman. Donald spent a sobering hour explaining exactly how to cut quarry tiles, using an angle iron, a cold chisel and a mallet. I found it hard to understand his broad Glaswegian accent, but reckoned I'd grasped the essentials.

That weekend, I experimented with Donald's method. The experiment was a total failure. Not only did my muscles again go into spasm, I wasted dozens of tiles and smashed my left thumb and most of the fingers of my left hand. Getting through *Feelin' Groovy* and *The Bleeding Banks of the Bleeding Ohio* on the guitar in Assembly the following Monday was top-order pain and I cursed Donald and his bloody angle iron and mallet. But maybe there is a God, for I was heartened by the sight of Donald in a similarly bad mood right after Assembly. While he had been working in the school's tiny triangular Library, where Sally had cut up the fuckin' books, Daryl the Bomber had climbed on to the roof and yet again prised loose the little glass slats of the skylight, to drop them one by one as near to Donald as he could get. Donald later told me that he had thought "the bleddie skule was fallin' apart". He had bustled outside to remonstrate with Daryl, who had retaliated by peeing on Donald from the roof. It's possible that Daryl had got the idea from my lesson on The

Crusaders and the Siege of Acre. But my children always went too far.

That night, I resolved to lose weight, learn some more guitar chords, and get someone else to cut the bloody quarry tiles.

10

Our first two teenage girls arrived in early December. Laura was thin and quiet, rarely but silently disruptive. Cheryl was loud, stomping down the corridor in her Cuban heels, and sounding like amateur talent night at the Buena Vista Social Club. We had been warned about Cheryl. She was said to have spread malicious rumours about a teacher at her last school, almost putting paid to the poor sod's career. I realised I should have to be very careful about how I behaved in front of Cheryl. There could be no holding of Ruby's hand, even as a joke.

Both girls joined Steve's group, and life became more exciting than ever at that end of the school. Laura and Cheryl spent much of their first morning at New Riverside in the girls' loo, halfway along the corridor, opposite the Library, doing their hair. With the exception of Charlie, another new arrival and much too sophisticated for this sort of thing, and Mike, who quite honestly couldn't be arsed, Steve's lads spent the first hour barging into the girls' loo and then rushing out as though pursued by Harpies. When that palled, Laura and Cheryl spent the next hour running out of the girls' loo and barging into Steve's classroom, hoping to provoke Simon, Larry and Jimmy into pursuing them back into the loo.

It proved an irresistible spectator sport for my group, but Cheryl had a tongue that blistered the ears, extreme even by New Riverside standards, and she verbally drove Terry, Daryl, Marianne and Anita back down the corridor to Room 2. Tom, of course stayed with me, to tell me over and over again that his dog had no nose. Cheryl came from the same children's residential campus as Anita, but from a different cottage. I think Anita was frightened of her. After one day, I know I was.

We now had sixteen children in the school, which Miriam must have considered a multitude, for she attempted to re-introduce religion into the school assembly. But again it failed. As soon as Miriam had started on "Oh, Lord, we thank you for this lovely day..." (it was pissing down outside), Anita, convinced that Miriam, with her eyes closed, was so fervently engaged in devotion that it was open house to misbehave, bestowed a lengthy V-sign on one and all, much as the Pope blesses the faithful from the Vatican balcony in Saint Peter's Square at Easter. There was a snigger from one or two present.

Miriam knew what was going on. The prayer ceased abruptly. "No one's laughing, Anita," she said, coldly dismissive, but then, sadly, she had to follow that immediately with: "Stop laughing, Cheryl."

Anita wriggled with a mixture of joy and fear, much as we shall all be doing at the Pearly Gates on Judgement Day. Cheryl told Miriam what she could do. Miriam told Cheryl what *she* could do, and we all joined in on the 'Amen'.

In the penultimate week of that first term our afternoon outings became more adventurous. Ruby and I discovered that it was possible to squeeze her group and mine into her van and my car. Our first joint outing was to Keston Ponds, roughly a twenty minute drive away, where we surprised the wildlife and annoyed the anglers. Unfortunately, Christmas holidays started early in Manchester, and Ruby's husband had come down in his sports car. He was younger, and fitter, and better built than I was, and I became scared when Marianne told him that I fancied Ruby - which was true, but as yet unvoiced by me.

"An' *she* fancies *him* an' all," said Marianne.

"Is it true?" bleated Tom.

I tried to explain that I thought Mrs Brinn was very nice, but that she was just a colleague, and it would be wrong to say that I fancied her. I was rather proud of that response, because it wasn't an outright lie. I didn't say I *didn't* fancy her, which would have been a lie, but used words which could be construed to mean that it would be improper to say such a thing, wrong in the sense of 'unwise'.

It was probably Anita who reported this exchange to Cheryl the moment we got back to New Riverside, just before going-home time. Cheryl clattered down the corridor to confront me.

"'Ere," she said. "You fuckin' fancy Miss Brinn. Yes, you do. Yes, you fuckin' do. You fuckin' fancy 'er!"

Another of the lessons that I was learning at New Riverside was that it is very, very, very difficult to lie successfully to maladjusted children. They have an instinct for what is true, a kind of in-built lie-detector. They sense what other people are thinking, and whether or not they're telling the truth. Barron labelled this ability 'outsight', to distinguish it from 'insight' - which most of them lacked.

I tried to smile at Cheryl, to appear at ease. "Now, I don't know where you got that idea from…," I started.

"Fuckin' obvious," she said, and clattered away.

Was it? Oh, dear.

All schools feel compelled to have Christmas parties, because preparing for it is that rare delight of being a complete waste of time. We decided that the children should have a proper Christmas Party, with games; and a Christmas tree with lights; and presents, Christmas crackers, and a visit from Father Christmas - a truly barmy idea.

Marianne and Anita spent hours making paper chains, and Daryl spent as many hours pulling the chains apart - but slowly, as if it was crueller that way, rather like Miles with the butterfly or whatever it was in *The Innocents*. Tom, dressed in mustard-coloured tights and a ginger jerkin, spent most of the day pretending he was running a restaurant. I'm not sure why. Every two or three minutes he'd hurry over to take my order, only to have his mind captured by something else, so that he forgot what he was pretending to do. Our exchanges became confused.

"What would you like to eat?"

"What have you got?"

"I dunno."

"Shall we write a menu, Tom?"

"Blimey! What for?"

"For your restaurant."

"What restaurant?"

I foolishly saw Christmas an as appropriate time to premiere my latest guitar hit in Assembly. It was Cecil Broadhurst's *The Cowboy Carol*, composed in the 1940s but then undergoing something of a revival. Miriam was delighted because it was truly religious; Ruby and the children thought it stank. I didn't like it; I've never liked any song that has an exclamation at the end of every line of the lyric.

Caught up in the wild Christmas spirit of sharing, Mrs Askew brought a huge box of buttons to school to show Sally. It contained dozens of different types of button - glass, pearl, fabric-covered, tortoiseshell, wooden, jet, etc. etc. It had taken Mrs Askew many years to amass the collection and Ruby reckoned it would take Mrs Askew several more years to re-collect, because Sally became over-excited and chucked the buttons all over the floor of the Home Economics room, the Library and the Hall.

The party began with a huge Christmas dinner, at which we were joined in the Hall by the psychiatric team, though they sat at a table apart. I hoped Knottingham-Forrest would pull crackers and put on a paper hat and look half human, but she didn't - bit of a delicate ego there, I reckoned. Straight after dinner, the children were taken out to the playground, which was used as a prison cage on this occasion so that they couldn't get back into the Hall to spoil everything before preparations for the party were complete.

We started with Pass the Parcel. With the exception of Tom and Sally, who had probably never been to any sort of party, the children knew what to do and how to cheat - pretending to drop the parcel on the floor in the hope that the music would stop during the considerably long time it took them to stoop and pick up the parcel, or snatching it back from the person to whom they'd just passed it, to give themselves a second chance of being in possession when the music stopped. Though we had more than enough parcels prepared, so that every child would have a turn to rip off the last layer of wrapping, synchronising a break in the music with suitable proprietorship of the parcel was always tricky, and fights broke out all round the ring of chairs. Each parcel was tightly bound with strongest quality ILEA sticky tape, so that the children had to work hard to unwrap it. The hope was that it would keep them sitting down for a long time. Maybe we overdid it. It took some children ages to peel off a single layer, while their mates shouted and swore at them to 'get a fuckin' move on'. Anita was so frustrated by the difficulties of unwrapping the parcels that she attacked them with her teeth. Micky's face was a picture of misery whenever he didn't win. Most of Steve's group adopted their customary air of haughty superiority. But they all took part, even Charlie.

'Musical Chairs' was a little too exciting. The smaller children were trampled by the DMs of Steve's lads. When there was only one chair left, Cheryl and Simon decided to fight for it rather than wait for the music to stop. 'Bobbing for Apples' was probably a mistake, but nobody was drowned. 'Statues' was surprisingly successful, mainly because nobody took any notice of the judges' rulings as to who had moved when they shouldn't have done, so everybody got a prize.

In the light of the violence that had preceded his entrance, Father Christmas must have put on a brave face, but you couldn't tell because he had four packs of cotton wool plastered from his eyes to the buttons on his cushion-packed scarlet cloak. Though some of the children believed that this apparition truly was Father Christmas, it was actually Dick the Driver. None of the children, not even those who travelled on Dick's bus, guessed that this was so, which created a problem. This extraordinary being, blood red, huge and ho-ho-hoing for all he was worth, was a stranger, and the children cowered away from him in fear. But then Father Christmas started calling all the adults 'sir' or 'madam' and Dick's cover was blown. Wild with relief, the children attacked him.

Steve, Ruby and I had each bought presents for the children in our respective groups. Funds were limited to 50p a head, so there wasn't much choice. What do you give a child who has nothing - including no enthusiasm, no self-esteem, and almost no aspiration? Ruby, Steve and I bought a selection of pens, torches, games and puzzles - all of which were immediately rejected by the recipients as soon as poor Father Christmas handed them over.

We played one last game. The hostel children went back to the hostel. The Croydon minicab arrived for Anita and Cheryl. The school bus departed, with Micky bestowing festive V-signs out of the back window. Happy bloomin' Christmas, everyone!

And yet... As I watched the bus turn into the road, an odd feeling of achievement came over me, so rare that it was a while before I recognised it. However much the children may have come to the party with hostile intent, they had taken part. It was a bit like that old couplet: 'And those who came to jeer, stayed to cheer'. They had had a school party. It was something they could refer to, to deride as they talked to any mates they had at home - the funny bits, the angry bits, the Father Christmas bits... and the good bits, the moments when one of the older children helped one of the younger ones, when one child was generous to another, when they all laughed at something genuinely amusing. They had not been left out. They had taken part.

Maybe I was trying to kid myself, but I thought they had perhaps learnt something that wild afternoon. It seemed to me that, though my expectations should at all times be of an educational nature, that phrase could be very widely construed. Literacy and numeracy were empowering and therefore important, but apart from that was it more important that our children learned what it feels like to be invited to share in something, and what it feels like to be accepted by others, and later to learn what it feels like to share and to accept others? One of Barron's wise sayings was that our children were all emotionally raw, and were existing at emotional ages way below their chronological ages. Our job was to identify roughly what emotional age they were operating at, treat them appropriately, and help them to mature. It made sense then. It still does now.

Nevertheless, the day after the Christmas Party - the last day of term - I felt profoundly grateful towards Miriam for deciding that all the children should go home immediately after school dinner. We had a brief and touching assembly in the morning, at which we all said 'goodbye' to Mrs Askew. It had taken Sally less than a term to drive her away. I think the melted wax crayons may well have formed some kind of fetish doll on which dear little Sally put some sort of curse. When Miriam announced that Mrs Askew was leaving, a ragged cry of 'Good!' went up from all but Tom, who turned to me and said: "You're not leaving".

"No," I said, wishing that I was Mrs Askew.

Ruby held out until the children had finally left and then burst into tears. I think Micky had nearly done for her. She was livid with herself for crying, and livid with him for making her cry. I'd no idea he was as stressful as that, but then he did tend to suck up to Steve and me - I suppose because he had no dad. It was very sad. Micky was very sad. They were all very sad, but they were also very infuriating.

As Miriam was teetotal, we sat in the staffroom drinking tea and coffee, and the term ended with a whimper rather than a bang. Under other circumstances I might have been profoundly relieved that the term had ended. But it was Christmas, and I hated Christmas. Sue's parents were due to visit us on Christmas Day, which meant that my parents would be in a bad mood because I wasn't going to visit them.

On top of that, my final image of this first term in my life as a maladjusted teacher was of Ruby and David driving off together.

11

Sue and I spent most of the Christmas holiday doing yet more work on our house. Lewisham Council had withheld a small portion of the mortgage advance, pending the completion of work they wanted us to do. Part of this was to re-point the brickwork on the chimney. The house was four storeys high at the back, where the cellar emerged at ground level, so the top of the chimney stack was more than twenty metres from the ground.

On a chilly New Year's Eve morning, a time when my head was full of ghosts, I took my bucket of mortar and my bricklayer's trowel, and climbed an extension ladder to the steeply-pitched roof. I had taken no safety precautions - no roof ladder, no climbing boards, and no rope fastening me to the stack. A little ice had formed on the slates. It would have been the perfect setting and opportunity for a suicide that looked like an accident. I wasn't in a suicidal frame of mind, but I was being very reckless.

Midwinter was always an emotionally difficult time. In the space of two months comes Christmas Day and the birthdays of both of my children. I had managed to maintain some sort of relationship with them for the first year after I left, but following a couple of visits to an empty house, I thought that my wife no longer wanted me to see them. A month without visiting was followed by another month, and another. By the end of 1971, communication had broken down completely. Apart from a small amount of information leaked by my mother, I had no idea how they were, what they did, what they liked, what they wanted for Christmas.

Each month I wrote out a cheque for the maintenance I paid to my wife for her and the children, and each month I experienced a slight feeling of relief as I posted it. I was at least fulfilling one obligation to my family. I don't think it helped that my bank account remained at Waterloo Station, as though I was some sort of Victorian cad, always on the point of fleeing to the Continent. On top of this, my relationship with Sue had lost its neo-teenage passion. After living with me for more than two years, she may well have realised that the maturity that had attracted her to me in the first place was more assumed than real.

Sue was living in a student world, mixing with another generation. After a day of lectures and tutorials, she wanted to dance, debate student politics, and go to the cinema; at the National Film Theatre I once slept through the entire three hours of Abel Gance's *Napoleon*, so to this day I have no idea who won the battle of Waterloo. We had different priorities. I didn't really care if one of her colleagues had been threatened with failure in his Fine Art Finals for submitting vast ink drawings of Chairman Mao, Che Guevara and Ho Chi Minh. I didn't want to discuss phenomenology (whatever it was). I was scared when she arranged for our cellar to store 10,000 copies of the then-banned *Little Red School Book*. After a day at work I didn't want to hatch plans for world revolution, I wanted to lick my wounds and sleep. I believed we had been in love with each other; whether I still was, I didn't know, and since I didn't know, presumably I wasn't.

I sat on the freezing roof, stretching forward to cram pellets of mortar into the gaps between the old bricks. Once or twice I nearly slipped. Or did I nearly jump? At that time, I wasn't, in the words of Barron, "in touch with my feelings", just like Tom and Terry and Duggie and Marianne and all the other New Riverside children. But I was beginning to suspect that at rock bottom, we're all maladjusted. Whether or not we can keep going is largely a matter of luck - and the more maladjusted we are, the more luck we need. Looking back on that day on the roof, I can see that I was far more maladjusted than I realised at the time.

I had mixed feelings about the approaching new term. The first term at New Riverside had been a mixture of exhaustion and excitement. Every day there had been the battle to keep my group under some sort of control. Every night I racked my brain to come up with tasks that were within their capabilities but were also educationally justifiable. Every day they were exhausted. Every day I was exhausted. The excitement was on several levels. It was exciting to be working in a brand new school with a brand new team. I'd never seen myself as part of a team before. At Preston House, I had been a left-wing thorn in a bed of Tory rosebuds; in Leatherhead, a wishy-washy progressive in a conservation area of ancient educational ideas; at Beulah Park, an ineffective Nicholas Nickleby. But at a maladjusted school, with suitable support from those on high, I might just fit in.

Key players among those on high were Mary Evans - our sympathetic inspector for the hostel - and Dr Snooper - our less than sympathetic inspector for the school. Snooper wasn't his real name, though his real name was also a synonym for 'spy'. He was a pompous, portly man, rather like Captain Mainwaring in *Dad's Army*. He was an infrequent visitor to the school because there was much in the ambience of New Riverside that didn't appeal to him. At the first signs of fists, fury or foul words, he would dash down the road to a nearby Junior School. To be fair, unless they were specialists in special education, it was difficult for inspectors to understand what was going on at New Riverside. We were trying to put into practice ideas that Dr Snooper wouldn't have accepted even if he'd understood them. We encouraged children to talk about their difficulties. We wished to identify the emotional level at which they were functioning, and then try to help them grow and mature. We wanted them to reach the point where they were able to see themselves through the eyes of others. We wanted to help them accept what had to be accepted. We wanted to convince them that they were capable of 'good' as well as 'bad'. It was exciting ('thrillin' in Barron's language) to learn how to do all this, and to perceive the first tiny signs that it was taking effect.

For a long time it was a matter of faith. Mary Evans and Barron told us what to do, encouraged us when we were feeling low (which was often), and heaped praise on us when we got it right. We needed much the same treatment as the children, and Mary and Barron supplied it. And, like the children, we needed time to work through all this - certainly more than one term - hence the exhaustion that went with the excitement.

At the beginning of 1972, in those last few days of the Christmas holiday, up on the icy tiles with the cold wind whipping round the chimney stack, pushing mortar into crack after crack, I thought about the coming term. Surely the future would be a little easier, a little kinder, a little more pleasant. I decided not to jump.

But the immediate future wasn't any of those things.

On the first day of term, Ruby, Steve and I greeted the children as they got off the bus. "Hallo," we said, hoping that it sounded as though we were glad to see them. "Did you have a good holiday?" One by one they barged past, all muttering "Fuck off!" save Tom, who said "Do you still love me?", and Duggie, who said "I had a smashin' holiday", which seemed a worrying symptom of normality.

New children were scheduled to arrive the following week, and a new teacher had already joined us. His name was Pete Thomas, and he was another graduate of Mary Evans' TOSLADIC course. Pete was friendly, quick to look for humour, and slightly camp. For three weeks he was to have no children while he sorted out his classroom and absorbed some of the atmosphere of the place. Three weeks seemed a generous amount of time to do the former but, for the latter, well, if you didn't absorb at least some of the atmosphere in five minutes, you never would.

Following Mrs Askew's departure at the end of the previous term, it had been decided to do away with Home Economics and replace it with 'Cooking'. Each group teacher would take his or her group for cooking one afternoon per week. It became one of my favourite pastimes at New Riverside. Cooking was a complete mystery to most of the children. In their experience, food came ready to eat. They didn't understand the notion of 'raw'. The following summer, we planted our little garden, a brave and somewhat foolish project, for the only area available was still covered with builders' rubble, and we had done nothing to feed and improve the soil. When the vegetables we'd planted struggled to a haggard maturity, the children couldn't relate what they saw to what they were used to eating. Little Sally gazed critically at the pea pods.

"Them ain't peas," she said. "Peas is round."

I didn't fancy going for anything too elaborate in Group 2's first Cookery session, so I opted for bread making. There were 10 loaf tins in one of the many Home Economics cupboards, and I figured that, if you use a loaf tin, it automatically makes something that looks like a loaf. I was wrong again. I hadn't realised how exciting the process of mixing ingredients was for our children, what a very tactile occupation it was.

Whenever Ruby's group cooked, Sally always asked "can you put yer 'ands in?". Pastry-making was popular for this reason, and kneading dough even more so.

With a large bowl each, a heap of flour, a jug of yeasty water and a large knife, we set about mixing our dough. The children didn't like the look of yeasty water ("it's like someone's gobbed in it...", "it's like your snot...") until the yeasty water started to bubble ("it's farting..."), and then of course they didn't want to mix it with flour. But I insisted, and eventually each of us had a pile of sticky dough to play with.

As we kneaded away, I explained the properties of yeast. The lecture wasn't going too well, because I didn't really know what I was talking about, so it didn't really matter when it was cut short by Tom. He was wildly over-stimulated by the warmth and the wetness and the sticky texture of the dough, and being encouraged to maul it about proved too much for him. I had tied an apron round him - he had protested at first, maybe thinking it was a strait-jacket - but the dough and flour flew from his hands, and covered his back, front, arms, trousers, hair and face. In the end, there was more dough on his shoes than in his loaf tin, and he looked as though he'd had to fight his way out of a windmill on a rainy day.

Nevertheless, the bread making was sufficiently successful for us to have another go the following Tuesday. Terry was a good cook, respectful of the process, quick to learn and not abusive of the ingredients. But I had to keep an eye on Daryl the Bomber, who stole bits of dough from the mixing bowls of the others while we were waiting for it to rise. To calm my chefs, I read aloud from the *Ladybird Well-Loved Tales*. *Rapunzel* went down very well, until Terry had a go at climbing up Marianne's hair. *Rumpelstiltskin* worked its usual magic, but I overdid the Ogre in *Jack and the Beanstalk* and had a coughing fit. Nevertheless, the loaves were even better than the previous batch, and it took less than twenty minutes to get Tom in a presentable condition to send home.

I made a couple of extra loaves, one of which I gave to Ruby when Cheryl wasn't looking. But one of my group (possibly Anita, possibly Marianne again, probably Daryl the Bomber) snitched on me, and dear Cheryl gave me a going-home time ear-bashing about "fuckin' fancyin' Miss Brinn".

"She's your fuckin' ex-wife," said Cheryl.

I didn't understand what she meant, but thought it better not to ask her to explain.

Two new children joined Ruby's group. Francis was eight years old, tall for his age and physically awkward - as though his joints needed tightening. Rumour had it that his mother had wanted a girl and had dressed Francis in girl's clothes. She'd even sent him to school in a dress, which I guess is hardly likely to give a lad a flying start in life. I just prayed that Tom didn't go back to wearing the cretonne frock, or poor Francis's fragile hold on his sexual identity would be shattered before he'd had a chance to settle in.

The other newcomer was seven-year-old Billy Andrews, an endearing looking child until he opened his mouth and revealed his teeth, which looked as though they'd been deliberately sharpened. Barron told us that Billy believed he had a *doppelganger* whom Billy called 'Billy Bandrews' - a naughty little boy who told untruths, didn't do his work, repeatedly lost his temper and was violent. Barron told us not to get involved with Billy Bandrews. I totally accepted his advice, having more than enough problems dealing with real trouble-makers without taking on phantom ones as well. On the second day after his arrival, I thought I heard Billy Bandrews having a tiny *contretemps* with Ruby, but couldn't be certain as Terry was shouting at Tom who had returned from his psychotherapy session with Barron a bit *agitato*, and was washing the Group's Maths books in the sink.

The weather was awful that January. There were many wet playtimes, nightmares to supervise. We took it in turns to look after the children in the Hall, where they swung on the ropes, and leapt from wall bar to wall bar. This involved clambering into perilous positions from which I expected them to plummet to their deaths or paralysing injuries, so that my career would be ruined and I'd be sued for a million pounds. That would inevitably mean prison, because I had only £18.03 stashed away at Waterloo. But the children didn't fall. They stayed on the ropes and the bars, defying me and gravity long after we should have started Assembly. At which point Miriam would come in and shout at them to get down, which they did, and then Miriam would give me one of her looks.

But gymnastics did produce one abiding memory of early days at New Riverside. We were in the Hall for what I grandly called a 'Gym Session'. Daryl the Bomber was swinging to and fro on one of the rope ladders, and Marianne was lunging sideways across his line of swing on another rope ladder. The plan was that at some stage she would launch herself from her ladder to join him on his ladder, rather as Gina Lollobrigida did with Burt Lancaster in *Trapeze*. It wasn't exactly the same, because Daryl the Bomber lacked some of Lancaster's dash (the awful spectacles didn't help), and Marianne looked more like Burt Lancaster than she did Gina Lollobrigida. Almost at the last moment, seconds before launch time, Marianne became aware that Daryl was flinching away from the *approchement*. She screamed at him.

"Daryl! Keep your legs together… I'm coming!"

Five days later, Donald the Handyman gave notice that he was quitting New Riverside and departed within the space of two hours. Matters had come to a head, literally, (no, honestly, I promise I'm using that word correctly) at yet another wet playtime when Daryl the Bomber snatched Donald's tam from his head, and ran off with it. In defence of Daryl, I should say that this was a difficult week for him as he'd been told that he was to leave Group 2 the next Monday and go to Mr Thomas (Pete) in Group 3. Barron had drummed into us how difficult our children found change, and how it was likely that old wounds were re-opened whenever they had to say 'goodbye' to someone who held an important position in their lives. It seemed to me that Daryl wasn't really saying 'goodbye' to Group 2, he was merely moving a few metres up the corridor. I also doubted that I occupied any important position in his life - other than that I might possibly have loathed him more than anyone else did. But I accepted that, whatever I thought, Daryl might well regard what was happening as rejection in a way. It's also quite possible that Daryl sensed my relief that he was going.

That night, I resolved to try to lose weight, to learn some more guitar chords, and to love the children that I instinctively disliked.

Late in January, Pete's group was officially launched with Daryl the Bomber and a newcomer, Ellen. She was ten-years-old, thin as a hazel switch, and permanently shaking like an aspen. She had a squeaky little voice which took much of the sting out of her swearing and profanities. There was the usual promenading up and down the corridor to examine Ellen and to see 'Thomas', as Pete was labelled by the children, at work. Members of my group (save Tom) were instantly convinced that he was a much better teacher than me. So was I.

Ellen had little contact with her parents, because she lived in a children's home in in south-east London. Kenny, who joined Pete's group a week later, was also from a children's home, but that wasn't true of most of our children. The majority lived with both parents. A broken home doesn't automatically cause maladjustment, nor is it an essential ingredient in the process by which a child becomes maladjusted. Some of our most unhappy children lived with both mum and dad, parents who were upset and frightened by their children's disturbed and disturbing behaviour.

We were told that Kenny was 12 years old, but I think this was his average age, as he managed to look both 6 and 18 simultaneously. Kenny could suck his thumb, pick his nose and smoke a cigarette simultaneously *using only his right hand*. With talent like that he should really have been in cabaret, and it occurred to me that there were many similarities between my job and a career in showbiz. Teaching is like being on stage all the time, putting on a performance in front of a hostile audience, sweating your guts out to win them over, having to do two shows a day, and knowing you have to be back on stage the next day even if they booed you and pelted you with rotten fruit and veg. I wished I could tap dance, or juggle, or eat fire, or do the Indian rope trick, or had any one party piece that would leave them gasping for more. I also wished I could do more than one thing at a time with my right hand, instead of feeling like a wanker most of the time. For almost a week, I flirted with the idea of learning how to do a knife-swallowing act, for its telling theatricality. I could start with a craft knife and work my way up to the big knives in the Cookery Room. But I knew my nerve would fail me long before the last minute, that such a deed might put silly ideas into the children's heads, and that anyway they'd probably be looking the wrong way at the crucial moment.

On one of Group 2's cooking afternoons, Ruby paid us a visit. We were making apple pies. I was a little tense because I wasn't too happy about the idea of Tom having a knife, so I was peeling his apples as well as mine. At my stupid suggestion, the other children were all throwing bits of peel over their shoulders to see what letter the peel made, for I had told them about the superstition that the peel would form the initial letter of the name of the person they'd marry. Every piece of peel seemed to form the letter 'S', so Terry told them that the 'S' stood for 'shit' and that was because they were all shit and they'd all marry shit.

While this was going on, Ruby sidled up and began nicking my slices of peeled apple and eating them, looking at me challengingly, like the children did when they were not really interested in doing something naughty but merely wanted to see if they could make you lose your temper. But, before I summoned up the courage to lose my temper, Mrs Gilbert, the School Secretary, came in to give Ruby some petty cash. The procedure was that, the day before we cooked, we went shopping with our groups to buy the ingredients, handing over the receipts to Mrs Gilbert, and the next day, Mrs Gilbert brought us the money we'd spent. On this occasion, she was paying Ruby a little over £5.

Mrs Gilbert handed the money to Ruby, and left. Ruby stood there, eating my slices of apple, with a fiver in her hand. Enter Larry, from Steve's group. He stood there, politely chatting to Ruby and me for a couple of minutes - what were we cooking, how were the new kids getting on in Ruby's group, that Thomas bloke was all right - pleasant conversational stuff, and then he left. Only after he'd gone did Ruby realise that, during the chat, he'd nicked the fiver from her hand.

A part of me thought it served her right for stealing my slices of apple (though in those days you could get hundreds of slices of apple for a fiver and she'd eaten barely half a dozen or so). Another part of me was grateful, because it meant I didn't have to lose my temper with her. Like many teachers, I could lose my temper only with children.

12

Throughout my years as a teacher, I had a special fondness for each February half-term. It always seemed to me that it marked the end of the worst of the winter. In our small garden, the forsythia was in bloom, and crocuses were poking through the dark earth. It was a time to think of buying packets of seeds, a time when the sap was rising.

We started the new half term with a new admission. Christina was fourteen years old, tall and slim. It had been decided that she should go to Ruby, to turn Group 1 into what we called a 'family group', with children across the age range. Ruby had been having a hard time with her very mixed infants, and it was hoped that an older member of the group would supply some stability. We believed we had collected enough evidence to show that older children profited from being with younger ones, as it gave them legitimate access to the toys and play apparatus that they secretly craved. I welcomed Christina's arrival in that it might put Cheryl's nose so out of joint that she wouldn't swear at me quite so often.

There were now twenty children in the school, the majority of them day pupils, so widely scattered across London that it was impossible for one school bus to collect them all. We were allocated a second ILEA bus, driven by Fred, a kindly soul and the dead spit of Corporal Jones in *Dad's Army*. Mrs Harrison, the attendant who rode shotgun on his bus, was also old, but had none of Fred's chirpiness. She was a moaner, and the children did not take to her. This mattered. The drivers and bus attendants played an important part in the everyday life of New Riverside. If the bus journey to school was happy, the children arrived in a settled state. If it wasn't, they arrived angry and distressed, and the day got off to a bad start. Similarly, at the end of the day, it helped if any good feelings the children had were re-enforced and any bad feelings weren't. Madge was good at this; Mrs Harrison, with her ungenerous attitude towards the children, wasn't interested. She didn't like them, which was wrong but understandable, and I suspect that she thought the children didn't deserve what she regarded as privileged treatment, which was also wrong, but wasn't understandable.

Going-home times worsened. So many children, even relative newcomers, didn't want to leave at three o'clock every afternoon that we came to suspect that anyone eager to go must have been nicking things and wanted a quick getaway. Rubbers and Plasticine were popular, so were screws (usually the ones that attached the fire extinguishers to the walls), and sanitary towels from the girls' loo. Sanitary towels intrigued males of a certain age at New Riverside; I think the age was eight. They had no idea what these strange objects were for, but experiment is often the pathway to knowledge, so they experimented. A newcomer to Ruby's group, on the customary New Arrivals' Curiosity Tour, popped into the girls' loo, and skipped merrily out with a sanitary towel on his head, the loops fastened over his ears. He ran down the corridor emitting a whirring noise. When questioned, he explained that he thought the towel was some kind of flying helmet, and he was pretending to be an air ace.

Going-home time on Friday was an extra tricky time. The children knew that the weekend meant they wouldn't be back in school for 66 hours (I'd counted them, even if they hadn't), and this made them cross. It also meant that the hostel children joined the day children on the buses, so getting home took much longer. With a bit of luck and bribery (not real money, you understand - I'd tried that and it didn't work), it was usually possible to coax Dick and Madge's passengers onto their bus, but sometimes Fred and Mrs Harrison's passengers had to be helped on board, rather like rush-hour commuters into Japanese bullet trains.

Once the buses had pulled away, Pete, Ruby and I freaked out. We behaved like the children. We swore. We threatened. We slammed doors. We threw things about. We chased each other up and down the corridors, skidding round corners and shouting 'fucker-bugger!' at the tops of our voices. Once or twice we wondered aloud to each other whether this indicated that we were becoming increasingly barmy. We took our worry to a Tuesday meeting, and were relieved to hear that such behaviour was common to people working under stress. Thus reassured, the following Friday we let rip with our 'fucker-buggers', to the surprise of Dr Snooper, who arrived to pay an unscheduled visit. But all he did was run away.

Special Education has often been wrongly presented as education for the weak, the handicapped, and the outlawed. This has led to parents resisting the idea of their children being consigned to such a world. In the 1970s and 1980s, if a child was declared in need of special educational provision, the Education Authority had the power to compel parents to send their children to special schools, though that power was seldom used. Persuasion was brought to bear, an informed and well-meaning persuasion, and much time and care was spent in its application. To Miriam's credit, she never tried to hide what was going on in her school, nor to hoodwink prospective parents. New Riverside was open to inspection. Parents were always shown round a working school, and I can remember only one set of parents turning us down. Our fingers were often crossed as parents made their guided tour, but our children usually rose to these occasions, displaying some quaint and eccentric ways, but seldom acting out. To the credit of the parents that came to us, I think they adopted a generous attitude towards New Riverside. It may well have been that they had seen much the same problems presented by their own children as they saw presented by ours.

The days were beginning to lengthen noticeably. It was now almost light when we came out of the Tuesday meeting. Though New Riverside was settling down, there was a permanent need to check the fine tuning of the establishment. Because there were enough older boys for competitive games of soccer at playtime, it meant that the younger boys and all the girls didn't get much of a look-in. Cheryl, Laura and Christina didn't seem to mind. They spent most of their playtime fixing their hair, but Anita and Marianne were understandably rebellious. Little Billy came to our aid by devising alternative entertainment, initially for Francis and Sally and Micky, though others were later welcomed. He formed a private militia - his dad had been in the Army - and drilled them each morning up and down the patio area by the sandpit outside Ruby's room. There was something of the Light Operatic about Billy's Private Army. Not only was he into toy soldier drill - that scarlet coated, red-cheeked, stiff arm and leg marching that is about as menacing as the approach of a teddy bear - Billy was even more into military wardrobe. He loved the dressing-up part of playing soldiers, though he became less enamoured of things military when it was explained to him that 'uniform' meant wearing the same sort of cardboard and crepe paper busby as the rest of his troops.

Micky was in raptures, for he was obsessed with war and battles. Whenever he got the chance, Micky devoted his time in the classroom to drawing little pictures of little men with little guns firing little lines of dashes (I think they represented bullets) at each other and dying little deaths.

One playtime, Billy generously handed over command to Micky.

"Right, Billy," said Micky. "You can be my lef'tenant, an' Sally, you can be my right tenant."

Francis, who must have welcomed a soldier's uniform as a change from having to dress as a girl, was much impressed by Billy. One morning, he sat down in his usual quiet way and worked on a large sheet of blue sugar paper with a poor quality blue ball point pen, to produce a picture that he nervously presented to Ruby. You had to tilt it a bit, until the light struck it from the side, to see what it was. It depicted a tiny stick figure in the bottom left corner and a tiny golden circle at the very top of the paper. A long dotted line connected the figure and the circle. The caption read: 'Billy is touching the snu (*sic*) with his willie'. It was a fine concept, and one that still cheers me occasionally on cold and gloomy days.

Sally still had her problems with Miriam – or maybe it was the other way round. One morning Sally arrived at school shorn of the wonderful copper ringlets that had made her look like an infant Mary Pickford. Her mother had decided to cut her hair, punitively - it looked as though it had been done with a machete. Sally was acutely conscious that all eyes were on her in assembly, and Miriam couldn't resist a jibe.

"I don't think much of your haircut, Sally," she said, as we settled down to close our eyes and put our hands together.

"Well, you'll 'ave to fuckin' lump it," said Sally.

In my list of Brave Moments I Have Witnessed in Life, Sally's response to Miriam's gratuitously snide remark stands alongside the moment when Sally had disputed with Miriam as to whose 'fuckin' school' it was. And, to Miriam's credit, she attempted no come back and didn't seek to have the last word. I think these things matter in education. There is a time to speak, and a time to be silent, even if you're the Head of a school.

Problems remained in Group 2. I was still having trouble with the last ten to fifteen minutes of each session of the day, just before milk time, just before dinner time, and especially just before going-home time. I thought I'd solved it when I came up with the idea of a virtual reality treasure hunt (though in those days we had to be content with sugar paper and wax crayons rather than high quality CGIs). One of my few talents was drawing freehand maps from memory. When I was little I used to trace maps from a pocket atlas, and then colour them, thereby creating a poor and totally unnecessary copy of the pocket atlas. Some twenty-five years later, this hitherto meaningless process was at last to be of use.

On a large sheet of sugar paper I drew a map of The World, or Europe, or the Pacific, or whatever, and then divided it into squares. Each child (or 'pirate' as they preferred to be called) was given a small piece of cardboard on which was written 'Flint' or 'Blackbeard' or 'Rackham Jack' or 'Kidd' (or 'Bonny' or 'Read' in the case of the girls). These cardboard pirates were then placed on pre-arranged points on the map, equidistant from the grossly out of scale Treasure Island (in the middle of the map) in terms of the number of squares. They all had to start from different points (or ports) otherwise there was considerable confusion, and race their cardboard galleons to the Island. The totally false premise was that the first to arrive would get the treasure, usually some cheap sweets. God knows what damage I was doing to their pirate teeth. It was a wonder they could still hold cutlasses in their mouths.

The speed of their voyage to the Island was determined by how well they answered questions in Maths ('What is left from 10p if you buy a banana for 5p?'), Spelling ('What's the first letter of the word Pencil?'), General Knowledge ('Which is bigger, Keston Pond or the Atlantic Ocean?'), and Current Affairs ('What is the job of the lead character in the song *Ernie - the Fastest Milkman in the West*?' - a Benny Hill song, very big in 1971). The problem was that every pirate had to get every answer right, because all pirates had to arrive at the Island simultaneously, so that each one of them plundered 100% of the treasure. Failure to achieve this synchronicity resulted in inter-pirate warfare, often the only realistic part of the whole operation. Some may regard the promotion of buccaneering as an abuse of educational authority, but it did keep children in the classroom.

And, over the months, there was evidence of Pirates' Progress. By midsummer they were required to answer questions on Natural History (Q: 'What animal has a hump?' A: an elephant, apparently), Sport (Q: 'In what game do you have a bat?' A: tip and run, which was fair enough, for we played it every day in the summer), and Science (Q: 'Which of these is the odd one out? Gold, silver, iron, or stinging?' A: stinging - all the rest are metals, stinging is nettles).

The second term at New Riverside came to an end. To my immense relief, the balance of the mortgage arrived from Lewisham Council. I calculated that in only another twenty-four years and seven months and four days (8983 days in all), the mortgage would have been paid off, and that I would then be 54 years old, and still teaching. Both my calculations were wrong.

13

It may have been the weather, for day after day the spring of 1972 was bright and blue and beautiful. It may have been a by-product of the emotional turmoil at the heart of working with maladjusted children. Whatever the reason, within a few weeks of the beginning of my third term at New Riverside, I found myself deeply involved with two people. One was Ruby, the other was an eight-year-old new pupil named Leroy.

We had been through Leroy's history at a Tuesday meeting the previous term. He had come to England from Antigua as a three-year-old in the mid-1960s, with his mother and his two older sisters. Mum got a job as a cleaner in a hospital, and Leroy's sisters went to school. Leroy was left alone all day in a flat in south London. One day, he found a box of matches and started a fire in the flat. He wasn't hurt, and the fire wasn't a big one, but when Mum discovered what had happened she was terrified. From then on, she strapped Leroy into a chair every morning, just before she went to work, leaving one arm free, with food and water within reach. This was not done out of cruelty, but simply because she had no idea how else to keep him safe and out of trouble. She had no friends or relations in London, no one to turn to. Eventually, she got to hear of Social Services or, more accurately, Social Services got to hear of her. By the time New Riverside got to hear of the family, Leroy had already been taken into care and was in a local children's home. He saw his mother infrequently, and it sounded as though they were both afraid of each other.

Miriam, with the usual head-teachers' preparedness to leave their own school as often as possible, had visited Leroy at the Junior School that was about to exclude him. She described to the Tuesday meeting how Leroy spent his days there: lying on a mat on the classroom floor, playing with toys, dozing sporadically, occasionally being patted by other children as they passed by. He had become the class pet - but at least he was no longer tied up. It was reported that he was regularly aggressive, but the Junior School could not see why. This was the reason they wanted to get rid of him.

I have phrased that harshly; it may be fairer to say 'this was why they wanted Leroy to have special educational provision'. There were times at New Riverside when all the adults became angry with mainstream schools, especially junior schools, which so often seemed to us to hold on to distressed and disturbed children far too long. Some schools regarded it as a matter of pride that they had held on to a child who presented serious management problems. Others feared that excluding such a child might reflect badly on them. Consequently, some junior schools went to absurd lengths to contain such children, so that the child's crisis was postponed until he or she reached secondary school. Scarcely literate or numerate, these children would flounder in the secondary environment, moving from teacher to teacher for each specialist subject instead of having just one class teacher, and even having yet another teacher or two in charge of their pastoral care. Once referred for special education at the age of 12 or 13 or even older, such children often waited another eighteen months to two years before suitable places were found. Pending such a transfer, these children sank into an educational limbo in which they failed more and more, and where the passage of time meant that they arrived at adolescence mightily frustrated and bitterly unhappy. The special education market was stuffed with teenagers who had been excluded from school (often more than one school), who now had multiple conduct disorders, but who were less than two years from school-leaving age.

The original idea had been that Leroy should join Ruby's group, as he was young and very immature. At the Tuesday meeting, however, it was decided he should come to me. Leroy's dad had never had anything to do with him, and the only family life he had known had been with his mother and his two older sisters. Leroy lacked adult male figures in his life, apart from stern Mr Oakes, superintendent of The Beeches, Leroy's children's home. I was too busy, too desperate, too dumb, and too full of my own guilt to appreciate the irony of being appointed substitute father. When it was settled that Leroy would come to me, the meeting came to an end - a little later than usual, at about a quarter to six. A couple of hours later, David, Ruby, Sue and I went to a Turkish restaurant in Deptford to celebrate Ruby's birthday, due the next day.

When male pigeons are desperate to mate, they scuttle around in circles, scraping their tail feathers along the ground, puffing out their chests and necks, and making little nods with their heads. It looks silly and displays a distinct lack of intelligence, because most of the time, female pigeons simply ignore them. My behaviour in the spring of 1972 wasn't much better. Cheryl had been right all along. I did fuckin' fancy Miss Brinn and, though I hadn't scraped my tail feathers on the path to her front door, there had been a couple of times in the Easter holidays when I had scuttled there in my best flairs, hoping that David was away. On one of these visits, I clumsily attempted to kiss her. She thought that, unlike a male pigeon, I was just fooling about, so we had not fallen into each other's arms and indulged in a steamy exchange of physical passion, which was a shame, because I wasn't kidding.

Ruby lived in the upper reaches of a large Victorian house belonging to Nobby, a choleric, chaotic, Communist metalwork teacher. Nobby spent his spare time in the street, dismantling old cars – which was why my tail-feather flairs were so greasy and dirty by the time I reached Ruby's flat. After working all day in a crazy school, Ruby spent all evening in a crazy house. Nobby had four children: three huge lads who constantly fought each other, and one daughter, who spent as much time as she could with Ruby, to get away from her brothers. Her ambition was to be excluded from secondary school and sent to New Riverside, where she could be with Ruby all day.

The trip to the Turkish restaurant was a baffling evening. I remember David being surprisingly witty, and Sue being surprisingly subdued. I thought she might be suffering from a surfeit of phenomenological empiricism - I know I was. I took care not to drink too much as I had to be up early next morning to take my Mini Traveller for a service at a local garage. Ruby said she would meet me there and drive me on to school.

The garage was roughly half a mile from New Riverside, much too near to be safe, but as I got into her A35 van, I wished her 'Happy Birthday' and gave her a friendly kiss on the cheek. She then kissed me, and then we kissed each other. Bits of words and broken phrases came out of my mouth. Ruby said we had better have a talk after school, which seemed reasonable - after all, as we were asking the children to get in touch with their feelings by talking, as adults, Ruby and I should do the same.

My legs were shaking when we reached school and I nearly fell over as I got out of Ruby's van, but once the children arrived, it was impossible to do anything but concentrate on their needs and demands. The day dragged on, with the usual spitting and arguing and exhausting attempts to be good (on the children's part). At last three o'clock arrived. With my legs still shaking, I got into the van and we drove round the corner from the school, parked, and talked.

It was a long talk, a sort of case conference about the two of us. Forty years later, I can remember only one contribution I made to the meeting and hence to the decision taken at the end. I told Ruby that I 'fancied her' - now, where could I have got that phrase from? It was certainly a phrase I had never uttered before in my life and one that sounded about as romantic as offering her a liquorice bootlace (two for a penny at the sweetshop). The decision reached was that we should embark upon 'a sordid little affair'. In agreeing to this, I was attempting to play it cool. What I didn't know was that Ruby was doing exactly the same. We were both putting on a veneer of sophistication to hide what a lawyer might have called our 'joint-and-several vulnerability'.

Where was this sordid affair to take place? Secrecy (my clumsy speciality) was of the essence, and it seemed both morally wrong and too dangerous to use either the house in Ladywell or Ruby's flat in Sydenham. Sue's comings and goings as a student were irregular and unpredictable; and David had left Manchester and moved in with Ruby. For a while, the 'sordid little affair' remained a mere concept.

Then, on the last Saturday in April, Sue and her college friend Linda (our ex-landlady from the floorless flat in Brockley days) decided to throw a party at our house. I think Sue was keen that I should build up a circle of friends more my own age. I had deliberately lost contact with my contemporaries when I left Epsom, and I was becoming something of a social embarrassment by repeatedly falling asleep within an hour of arriving at undergraduate parties. So Sue encouraged me to invite Ruby. It was an uncomfortable evening. I clumsily tried to hold Ruby's hand under the table, so that we both ate one-handed and kept dropping bits of food. Later in the evening, I came across Ruby on the floor in the living room, listening to the allegretto from César Franck's *Symphony in D Minor* - which, as Nigel Tufnell rightly says, is the saddest of all keys. Ruby looked miserably up at me and said: "If ever we do go to bed together…" Others came into the room and she couldn't finish the sentence, but there wasn't really any need to.

On Monday morning we were back at school, with our faces well and truly in the shit, and with another new customer for Steve's group. This was Richard, a good-looking but awesome (in the true sense) thirteen-year-old who brought fear to almost everyone in the school. The adults already knew from the papers on Richard that he had almost succeeded in an attempt to kill himself a few months earlier, and somehow, probably from Richard himself, the children soon got to hear of this.

The news terrified them. For all their careless bragging and their tough talk and veneer of heartless composure, they were extremely sensitive, and just as frightened of death as they were of life. Not long before Richard's arrival, a neighbour of little Sally - an old woman - had died. This was Sally's first encounter with the fact that none of us goes on forever, and she found it very hard to understand. Throughout the morning she said nothing about this, but waited until we were all having dinner in the Hall. Sally was never a big eater; she used to nibble at bits of lettuce or a single chip or a grain or two of rice pudding. That day she ate nothing, but waited until the moment when Ruby was serving second helpings of jam sponge and custard to voice her fears.

"Miss," she said, "an old lady in our flats died..." What became clear was that Sally wanted to know what death was, what it meant.

Ruby's first thought was 'what the hell do I say?' As a good atheist, she knew better than to fob Sally off with some story about Heaven and Life Everlasting, so she explained in simple terms what happens when someone dies and that it happens to everyone.

"Will it happen to my mum?"

Ruby told her that it would.

"Will it happen to me?"

These are tough questions, and the temptation to skirt around them is great. Ruby's sister Maureen - who later joined us as a teacher at New Riverside - used to say that the truth could hurt but could never damage. I'm no authority on telling the truth. A Public School education not only taught me the advisability of lying at critical times but also how to do it (you can see the same trait in leading British politicians throughout history). But I do believe there are times when a distinction needs to be made between telling the truth and being honest. And Ruby drew on her honesty to answer Sally's questions. It was upsetting for them both, but Ruby had immediately realised the importance of telling Sally the inescapable fact about death - that it really is an end. Simple deceit about the universal (rather than the particular) was probably never the origin of any of our children's distress or disturbance, though it may well have become a later contributory factor. There were often times when I was caught off guard by a direct question that I had not expected. One day, early in her career at New Riverside, Marianne asked me if the sex act was painful 'the first time' for a woman. I should have paused and collected my thoughts before replying. How did I know whether or not it was for a woman, for a young girl? I should have had a word with Ruby, or better, I should have suggested to Marianne that Ruby was the person to ask. Instead, I said that it wasn't. I didn't know what I was talking about, but the default setting, if not the instinct, is always to be protective, to reassure children that everything is, or will be, OK. Failing that, I should have kept my mouth shut.

In the case of death, Richard would have known more about it than I did. He was someone who had flirted with death, looked it in the face, and had attempted the ultimate action which denies adults the chance to help, to intervene, to try to care, to make life better. I never heard Richard talk about his suicide attempt, and we never mentioned it, though I'm sure the subject was discussed in his psychotherapy sessions with Barron. But Richard knew that we knew it was part of his repertoire - an act that he might be prepared to revive. It coloured any exchange with him. Much of the time he behaved reasonably, worked steadily, and was coldly polite. But he was an expert at making you angry, while he remained calm and appeared supercilious. He openly mocked the school: we didn't know what we were talking about; we were all mouth and no action; we did nothing to help him. Every day, other children hurled similar accusations at us, but in rage and despair. With Richard the accusations were always made in a chillingly controlled voice.

After death, there is life. Two days after Richard's arrival, Ruby and I left school separately, as soon as was decently possible following the children's departure, and went to bed with each other. I am still ashamed that I... that I did what?... Did the dirty on Sue? Betrayed her? Committed adultery? In comparison, how easy life must be for pigeons. I was very frightened of going to bed with Ruby. In my mind it was a bit like throwing myself off a roof. I wanted her so much, and I wanted our making love to be as powerful as my craving for her. Well, it wasn't. It was far more powerful. And so much more overwhelming than jumping off any roof could ever be.

14

It was weeks before Ruby and I again went to bed together. Instead, we went to a wood a few miles to the south - I'm not going to say where as it's a deeply secretive part of my life. The wood was small, secluded, and carpeted with bluebells. We discovered it quite by accident one day after school, when we were looking for a country pub in which to have an illicit drink. Beneath the trees was an undergrowth of soft young bracken. Several late afternoons that warm and wonderful May, we lay together among the bluebells, making love and being bitten by a variety of blood-thirsty insects. Once or twice, we wondered if we might raise our heads from our passion to find a police officer standing there, notebook (or perhaps sketchbook) in hand, or worse, a Puritanical farmer, shotgun in hand. But we were lucky. We were never disturbed. If anyone did see us, they left us alone.

After making love, we lay side by side for an hour or so, gazing through the young boughs and the uncurling leaves at the blue sky high above us. Then, reluctantly, we remembered who we were and where we were supposed to be, leapt up, brushed the bits of leaf and twig from our bodies, dressed quickly, and drove at speed back to our respective homes. From one perspective, what we were doing was shameful. Ruby was married; I was supposed to be in a stable relationship with a very young partner. The woods were open to the public - and to those beautiful skies, which was one reason why what we did there remains unforgettable. From another perspective, what we were doing was sharing a love and a passion that has remained to this day. And, yes, we have been back to that bluebell wood, and we still weren't caught.

We did what we could to keep our affair secret from everyone at school, especially the children. But Cheryl was always on the prowl, clattering in and out of our classrooms at every opportunity, accusing me of fancying Ruby - "yes, you do, you fuckin' do!" - and accusing Ruby of being my ex-wife. She was alone in this moral crusade. The other children were too involved in their own difficulties to pay much attention to Cheryl's accusations.

One Friday after school, however, Ruby and I dropped our guard. We had driven together to the parade of local shops to get to the bank before it shut at half past three. Our sordid little affair had become a great joy to us, and we couldn't resist holding hands as we waited to cross the road to the bank. What we had forgotten was that some of the hostel children now went home for the weekend by public transport, and that there was a chance that they might still be hanging around, waiting for a bus. We were caught. As we crossed the road, a loud cry went up from the bus stop - "Ho! Ho! Ho!" – and there was Duggie and Daryl the Bomber. Ruby and I hastily separated, and I thrust my hands deep into my pockets with almost masturbatory speed. But the damage was done, and we knew Monday morning would not be easy.

It wasn't. All was quiet until Cheryl's arrival from her children's home in Croydon. She came straight to the staffroom door just before school was due to start, with Duggie (the snitch) smirking behind her. Cheryl let fly. She had fuckin' known it all along. She had fuckin' said so. Nobody had fuckin' believed her. But they fuckin' would now, and she would fuckin' tell everyone.

She did tell everyone. And nobody believed her. She had cried 'wolf' so often that when it was at last true, not a blessed soul accepted what she said. I was convinced Miriam would throw a fit, that Ruby and I would be charged with professional misconduct, and that one or both of us would be sacked. Instead, Miriam gave Cheryl a ticking off. "Now, look here, Cheryl," she said, "remember what happened the last time you started spreading lies about people…" It stopped Cheryl in mid screech.

Later, Ruby and I learnt more about what had happened at Cheryl's previous school. She had accused one of the teachers of assaulting her. The poor man had professed his innocence, but Cheryl had persisted in her story until the very day when the case was due to come to court. Only then did she withdraw her accusations. She had lied, but everyone had believed her until then. This had been added to the list of reasons for excluding her from that school and sending her to us. And now, with truth on her side, nobody believed her.

I managed not to lie when she confronted me. I was not so much economical as miserly with the truth. With her voice rasping, she repeatedly shouted at me: "Well, go on then, are you fuckin' denyin' it? Are you sayin' you weren't fuckin' holdin' her hand?" And at each repetition one or other of two things happened. Either another adult intervened and said: "Now, come on, Cheryl. That's enough"; or I simply held my peace, and let Cheryl continue until she accused me of something I hadn't done. "Go on! You're married to her! She's your wife! Yes, she fuckin' is!" And then I could truthfully say: "Cheryl, of course I'm not married to Mrs Brinn."

I wasn't proud of this technique then, and I'm ashamed of it now. All I was being accused of was holding Ruby's hand to cross the road. Even forty years ago I doubt I'd have lost my job for that. So why didn't I admit it? Because… because…

because, not only had my world of secrecy been invaded, but something very childlike inside me was scared that life was once again reeling out of control. I had deserted my wife and children. I was living with a former pupil. I was having an affair. Where would my funny little winkle lead me next?

But the technique of simply making no plea in response to the accusation worked. One of the few things that distinguished teachers from children at New Riverside was that we had sufficient self-control and self-esteem not to react to the jeers and allegations hurled at us. Self-esteem is often at its most effective when it's used for nefarious purposes. The children, having almost no self-esteem, always rose to the bait of a jeer or an accusation, no matter how ridiculous. The classroom would be quiet. The children would be working. All would be peaceful. And then one child (Marianne was very good at this) would turn to another and say: "Your mum gets all your clothes at Tesco's". Immediately - chaos. Fights. Abuse lobbed to and fro. Chairs flying through the air. Tears. Doors slamming, windows breaking. Work torn up by the child whose work it was.

And it was so often a remark about someone's mum. "Your mum's a slut... a whore... a tart... a witch... a bitch... a spastic..." "Your mum smells." "Your mum's had more pricks in her than a dartboard." Even, after the *Herald of Free Enterprise* disaster at Zeebrugge in March 1987, "Your mum's dead in the ferry." Whatever was said about 'your mum' always had the desired effect of producing violence and mayhem. In the end, a kind of Pavlovian reaction set in to the words 'your mum'. There was no need to go any further than that to start a fight. The stirrer would sit there and say 'your mum', and even those to whom the words were not addressed would oblige by ranting and raging and re-arranging the room. For there was a kind of trade union solidarity about the disorder in my classroom. If one child blew up, they all did; not always, but usually. They had a remarkable ability to tell when someone was genuinely (as opposed to theatrically) upset and then they would respectfully yield centre stage and wait patiently in the wings. But when it was a free-for-all, they were irresistibly drawn in.

As well as the awesome Richard, two other children joined us in May 1972. Tammy (lumberjack shirt, jeans, boots, and a boyish air) went to Pete's group. She arrived on the morning of Cheryl's *J'accuse* performance. Like most of our children, Tammy was used to seeing strange things happen in life and was nothing like as intrigued by such an incident as I would have been at her age. The other newcomer was bold, thirteen-year-old Derek Symes who established the record for Shortest Stay Ever at New Riverside. He arrived at 09.15, and departed at 10.20. In those 65 minutes he had shown no interest in settling in, and had then attacked Miriam with a saw in the Art and Craft Room. I'm not sure whether she was more cross than frightened, but her reaction was swift. She had him marched down to her room, and there she phoned his parents and told them to come and get him.

They drove up, and appeared not in the least surprised by what was happening. They listened to what Miriam had to say, which was a lot, but their only remark was that this wasn't much of a school. When they led young Derek out to their car, dad said to mum: "Well, that's another school under our belt", rather as though they were from the North American Plains and were in the process of assembling a collection of academic scalps. There were no protests. Derek came, he sawed, but he didn't conquer. I guess his papers followed him to another school or clinic or tutorial unit, from which he may well have been excluded in turn. If he had come to such an establishment as New Riverside say four or five years earlier, at the age of eight or nine, things might have worked out better for him, and for us. As it was, the drama of his rapid coming and going was upsetting for all our children.

With more pupils in the school I began to get a clearer picture of the child we could best help. Our speciality was those children who were emotionally disturbed rather than, or as well as being, gratuitously violent. Miriam had some latitude in deciding whom we'd take and whom we wouldn't. Once a term she attended Banding Meetings with fellow Heads of other ILEA maladjusted schools in South London. At these meetings, they discussed the dozen or so children awaiting placement. Miriam's preference was to pick the younger, bright but neurotic children. She wasn't too interested in fourteen- or fifteen-year-olds with plain old conduct disorders. Though this didn't go down enormously well with her colleagues or the Authority, it was in many ways reasonable. There was little any school could do to help teenagers who had only a year or two of compulsory education left. It takes time to help a child who is badly damaged by life, and with every passing year not in special education, any problems the children presented became more serious. Miriam had to take her share of such children - Derek was a case in point. He had arrived with rage in his heart and exhaustion in his eyes, asserting that he neither wanted nor needed our help. It was thanks to Miriam's tough line on taking adolescents that, in the first seven years of New Riverside, there were only four children we couldn't manage and who had to go.

Critics of special educational schools and units didn't then like, and probably still don't like the idea of depriving children of the wider curriculum available in mainstream education, but the problem is that, no matter how wide and wonderful the curriculum, some children are in so emotionally distressed a condition that they can't take advantage of it, and sending them to a mainstream school is largely a waste of time and resources.

Papers on children referred for special education arrived at New Riverside by ILEA internal post, as they did at the two schools with which we were banded. After consulting with the psychiatric team, we selected the children we thought we could help, and put the papers relating to the other children to one side. Miriam went off to banding meetings, and returned with good news or bad news or, usually, a mixture of the two.

Educational administrators didn't like our picky attitude. They wanted children placed in schools as soon as possible, as did the parents, politicians and pressure groups within the ILEA and the Greater London Council. All of which was perfectly understandable, but placing children in schools that can't help them is not only bad for those children, it's also bad for those schools and the children already there. The legal responsibility then placed on ILEA and local authorities to provide education for every child could only be effectively met if those authorities were given sufficient funds to cover whatever was needed, and the same is true today. Special schools are expensive to run, as are (or were) tutorial units and home education. If we judge a society on how well it looks after its weaker members, we should also judge an educational system, not just on how well it caters for its high flyers, but also on how well it meets the needs of those who may never fit comfortably into any school.

15

I don't know why or how Leroy immediately became special to me. No one else fell for his mixture of inept cunning, transparent raw emotion and naïve dishonesty. He was totally illiterate and, by New Riverside standards, not very bright. He was so out of touch with his own self that he often asked me to tell him how he was feeling: "Am I tired, Yakky?... Am I cold?" He was feisty, physically ready to take on all comers, except Marianne. He clearly identified me as the one person around less capable than he was, and liked to engage me in daily battles of wits: "Ha! Caught you out dere, see!" I suspect he was familiar with violence and probably with physical punishment. I once came across him in the corridor giving a hard-to-love lad called Jeffrey a hard time. Leroy was whacking Jeffrey's plump backside with one of our famous unbreakable rulers.

I assumed my outraged attitude. "Leroy, why on earth are you doing that!"

"Because it's nice," he said, for he could also be naïvely honest.

He was a hopeless criminal. When a gang from his children's home posted him as look-out while they raided an ice cream van, Leroy was the only one of the gang to be arrested. Early in his career at New Riverside, one of the children had a toy car stolen, which served him right, as the children were under strict instructions not to bring toys to school. Leroy was the prime suspect.

I went to him. "Leroy, why did you pinch Matthew's car?"

"What car?" he said, plunging his hand into his trouser pocket.

"The one in your pocket."

He was impressed, and immediately handed it over: "How did you know it was there, Yakky?"

At first, I didn't know what to do with him. He couldn't read, he couldn't write, he could just about form numbers and do the simplest of addition sums. He had no idea how to play with other children. With a limited hold on his own identity, he couldn't take part in any of Miss White's classroom theatrical productions, and became their sole audience, sitting with his mouth gaping open as the drama developed. Art didn't appeal. History was bunk. St Cecilia had not bestowed upon him the gift of Music. He longed to play football with the older boys but, like a toddler, his physical co-ordination was poor when it came to ball games - though he was swift and agile enough when I was pursuing him through the school and beyond.

But children at New Riverside often gave us clues as to how some sort of compromise could be reached in the educational process. It was our job to recognise these clues, and to distinguish between the false ones - the red herrings - and the ones that were intended to be genuinely helpful. And this was exactly what Leroy did. Within a matter of days, he had developed his personal timetable. Every morning, he leapt from the school bus, fighting the others to be first off, and raced into the classroom. He sat next to me, usually on my left, while Tom stuck to my right. For an hour or more, he honestly tried to make sense of the simple money and shopping sums I had set him, and tried to listen while I waxed lyrical on the wonders of culture and learning. After that hour, when Lil brought the milk, Leroy drank greedily from the little bottle (like a toddler, he called it 'bockle').

Heaven help us, there was always trouble if the 'black bastard' milkman had delivered cartons instead of bottles (the milkman wasn't black, nor a bastard - as far as I know - but in the 1970s black and white children alike used 'black bastard' as a cuss on both their black and white peers).

Every playtime, for a month or more, Leroy provoked a fight, sometimes with me, more often with another child. I waded in to restrain him, and he let me control him, though he always made sure this wasn't easy. Every day we wrestled our way down the corridor to the Medical Room, which was spacious and quiet and about as far from the hurly-burly as you could get in the school. Every day, I put him to bed, tucked up with plenty of blankets, and read him a story (his favourite was *The Three Billy Goats Gruff* - I like to think it was because of my gem of a reading as the Ugly Troll, but it was probably because he liked the violence on the footbridge which, let's face it, is far more exciting than Macaulay's *Horatius*). Leroy then slept until the end of morning school, when he woke ravenously hungry. He ate a huge dinner, and spent his afternoons in the classroom in comparatively peaceful play. At going-home time, I escorted him to Madge's bus, where Leroy and I usually parted on friendly terms.

Our Friday afternoon trip to the Baths was his favourite part of the week. He dashed from the bus to the changing room, chuckling as he tore off his clothes so that he could be first into the water ("Ha! Beat you dere, see!"). After swimming, I helped him dress, and he made a tremendous show of rubbing Nivea cream into his hands, which otherwise became dry and chapped. Then, if there was time for a visit to the nearby sweetie shop, Leroy was always first in the queue.

It was on one of these visits that I first realised that he had come to accept everything I said as Gospel Truth. As we passed the local fishmonger's, the children were attracted by a bucket of live eels in the window. They wanted to know what they were - "those great fat worms - ugh!" I explained that they were called eels and, since Sue wasn't there to condemn my value judgements (which weren't allowed on her Sociology course), I added that I thought the way they would be taken out of the bucket and slaughtered on the fishmonger's slab was cruel, though I may not have put it quite as brutally as that. We then studied all the other fish in the window - all of which were disappointingly dead as far as the children were concerned.

Leroy took my lecturette on eels to heart, and the next time we passed the fishmonger's, he said: "There's that cruel man, Yakky, and we don't like him, do we, 'cos he keeps live kippers in his window."

Like a very young child, he found it difficult to process information, to sort it into some kind of order, and this led to frequent confusion. One day he picked up a book called *Stories from the Bible* - a book I much disliked because the stories were fatuously recounted and the illustrations of the usual Old Testament tales of brutality were in the style of a 1950s advertisement for American toothpaste.

Leroy thrust *Stories from the Bible* at me. "Read us a story, Yakky," he said. The others gathered round.

"What story would you like?" I said.

"My favourite," he said, "'Ansel and Gretel.'"

One afternoon, as we hacked away at our pieces of blazer wood, the children started talking about their parents. Leroy had no idea of his own family background, and I thought it might be a good idea to sit down with him and attempt to construct some sort of family tree. I drew stick figures to represent Leroy and his sisters and his mum and his dad. He said he hadn't got a dad. I explained that everyone had a dad, even if they had never seen him. Then I drew stick figures to represent his grandparents, also unknown to him. He was amazed that there were four of them. Then I added his great-grandparents (eight in number) and his great-great-grandparents (sixteen). His mouth fell open.

I was worried that he might think he was a freak. "Everyone has sixteen great-great-grandparents," I said, "but they're almost certainly dead."

"When were they alive?" said Leroy.

"Oh, about a hundred years ago," I said.

He thought hard for a moment or two, counted his sixteen stick great-great-grandparents and said: "The world must have been a very crowded place in those days."

It was a totally logical remark for anyone who had no previous experience of how family trees work, as was Sally's question to Ruby when she looked up into the sky one morning and saw the Goodyear Airship silently cruising overhead.

"Miss, what time do it be up there?"

The summer term passed all too quickly. Its highlight was the Greatest Heist in the History of New Riverside.

A small army of women from the surrounding council estate worked in the hostel as cooks and cleaners. They were local mums, who probably knew more about children than anyone else at New Riverside. Once a week, Mrs Gilbert counted out their wages, popped the money into little bags which she then took across the driveway between the school and hostel to the Deputy Warden's office, where the Ladies (as they were politely called) collected their pay. The total sum involved was around £250 a week (with which you could have bought one thirtieth of an average price house in 1972, so by today's house price levels, today's cleaners at New

Riverside should be getting £7600 a week between them - but I bet they aren't).

I think it was in the second week of June that these wages went missing. One moment they were on Mrs Gilbert's desk, right in front of her; the next they had vanished, just like Ruby's fiver when she was nicking my apple slices. Nobody suspected an adult had been responsible. It must have been one of the children, but which one? There was a buzz of excitement in the air, but no child was behaving suspiciously. It couldn't have been one of Ruby's group; they were too young, too innocent, too incompetent. The only one in my group with a record of theft was Leroy, but this was far too big a job for him to pull. It had to be one or more of Steve's group, where excitement was at its highest.

Without a shred of evidence whatsoever, it would have been asking for trouble to accuse them, singly or collectively. All Steve could do was summon them together - they all came voluntarily - and invite them to sit down, as he had something very important to discuss with them. They sat down. He explained that some money had gone missing. There was an immediate outcry from a couple of them to the effect: "Are you saying we nicked it?" At such moments, you have to get in touch with your gut feeling - the brain is useless. Is this a sign of their guilt? Or is it a sign of their hoping they'll be judged guilty because they're actually innocent and it would put them in a powerful position if they were unjustly accused?

Steve proceeded slowly with his inquiries. This was brave, because he didn't have much time. The women from the hostel had agreed that the school had until going-home time to get the money back. If they didn't get their much-needed wages then, they would go to the police. Steve made no threats to search his group's desks or lockers (none of the children had a desk - there were only tables at New Riverside - and the lockers were open-faced wooden ones, without doors). He made no threats that searches of their persons would be carried out. He simply explained that we had to have the money back, not because of the police (he knew that some of his group would be wildly excited if the police were called in), but for the sake of the women workers. They had families to feed. They didn't have money in the bank, and they didn't have savings - which would almost certainly be the case now, despite what politicians and much of the Press would have us believe. He went quietly on and on, leaving them time to ask him questions and think about what had happened.

They did ask him questions. They were not saying they knew who did it, or that it was one of them, but they wanted to know what would happen to whoever had done it. Would the police be called? No. Would their parents or children's homes be told? No. Would they be suspended from school? No. The afternoon wore on. The rest of the school did not become involved. Most of our children had enough on their own plates, and anyway, they recognised and respected this as a genuine crisis. After the initial shock and *frisson* of excitement, Ruby's group and my group kept themselves to themselves, if for no other reason, because they sensed that, under these circumstances, they would get a rough reception from Steve's group if they shoved their noses in where they weren't wanted. Eventually, at about ten minutes before the deadline, Charlie said he wanted to have a word with Steve privately.

Ruby and I didn't know what had happened until after school, when all the children had departed on the buses or to the hostel. Steve told us that Charlie had confessed that he'd nicked the wages. Telling Steve to wait, Charlie nipped out, to return two minutes later with the money intact. Charlie was open and honest about what he had done. After he'd snatched the money from Mrs Gilbert's desk, he had gone to the Woodland Walk that ran at the back of the school, separated from us by a chain-link fence. The fence was broken in one or two places and Charlie had squeezed through, to stash the money under the exposed roots of a fallen tree. Steve counted the money. It was all there. Steve thanked him, which was the right thing to do. We had a result. More importantly, the cleaning ladies had their money. It was what everyone wanted to happen, including Charlie in the end. Over time, I came to see how important it is, in any conflict with a maladjusted (or any other) child to work towards what you want to happen. It's the adult's job to decide what he or she wishes the outcome to be.

The joint outings that Ruby and I arranged for our groups became more adventurous. Early in June, we took them in her A35 and my Mini to join her irritatingly ubiquitous husband David in Brockwell Park, Brixton. David was now working in an Educationally Sub-Normal School (how strange these labels now seem – Maladjusted School, Educationally Sub Normal School, Autistic School) in London, and not really enjoying it. He had arrived at an Inner London Education Authority school at a time when some members of the Greater London Council (GLC) were raising the issue of the inappropriate placement of black children in ESN schools. Many of these children were not educationally subnormal at all but, on top of the trauma of leaving their grandparents and their childhood friends in the West Indies, were merely having understandable difficulty in fitting into the culture of an educational system very different from the one back home.

During the outing to Brockwell, I began to see why GLC members were so concerned. David's school (predominantly white, correctly diagnosed, ESN children) was playing a cricket match against an ESN school whose pupils were primarily of Caribbean origin. The white children were un-athletic in build, had poor physical co-ordination, and knew little about how to play cricket. The black children were lithe, muscular and knew all you need to know about cricket, at that time indisputably the national game of most of the Caribbean. On that June afternoon, parts of Brockwell Park were terrifying places. Small white batsmen, oblivious to what was happening, stood bat in hand, sometimes holding the wrong end, and often facing the wrong way, as young Michael Holdings came pounding up to the bowling crease and sent down West Indian thunderbolts. I couldn't concentrate on the happy frolicking of our children while Death was only just-short-of-a-length away.

A couple of weeks later, we went to Chessington Zoo, where several of the children rolled up pieces of plain paper and pretended to be smoking (as a sign that they weren't frightened of the animals), and Leroy had his photograph taken sitting by the Irish Wishing Seat, his eyes tightly closed in recognition of the instruction notice - 'Sit down, close your eyes and Wish'. I so wanted to know what he wished for, but he wouldn't tell me. Other outings were to Knole Park, the Bluebell Railway, and the seaside. We picked a bad day for Camber Sands, a day of howling wind and lashing rain. As soon as the two ILEA buses drew up in the soggy car park, conflicting wants and needs were verbally and visually registered by all members of the party. Ruby let it be known that there was no way she was going to leave the warm school bus. Miriam agreed. Most of the older children looked hungrily at the Amusement Arcade and were promptly told by Miriam that it was out of bounds. Maureen, however, exhibited the sort of leadership that made Sir Ernest Shackleton so loved by his men throughout the wastes of Antarctica.

"Who's going to be first into the sea?" she called, and a small group of intrepid explorers followed her on to the enormous stretch of sand, Tom and I linked together bringing up the rear.

In silence, we fought our way against the gale force wind. There was no one else to be seen for miles around. When we had walked about two miles and were halfway to the sea, Tom looked up at me and indicated that he wanted to whisper. I bent my head.

"Are we allowed to shout here?" he said.

I said that we were, and he did, magnificently.

Having run away to the seaside when he was only four, Micky had form when it came to outings. He could turn any outing into an unhappy experience. His speciality was to wait until it was time to head back to school, and then trap himself somewhere - at the top of a pole, on a roof, with his leg caught in railings. Because of this thoroughly annoying habit, he was occasionally banned from outings, but the ban never lasted long enough as far as I was concerned. After missing one or at the most two outings, he'd be back on the bus again, with a big smile on his face and a packet of sandwiches in his hand, asking where we were going. And if he didn't go on an outing, he'd make trouble at school.

On one occasion, when Ruby's group and my group went to Toad Rock, near Tunbridge Wells - to practise being together nicely in public - Micky was left behind, in Miriam's care. This was because he had given us clear indication that he was not in a fit state to undertake such a dynamic expedition. He didn't accept this diagnosis and, once we had gone, he registered his anger by blocking the sink in Ruby's classroom, turning the tap full on, and flooding the floor to a depth of two inches. On our return from Toad Rock, Ruby discovered him, sitting in a chair, arms folded, with a look of sullen satisfaction on his face, like King Canute at the seaside. Micky continued to sit there, while Steve, Ruby, Lil Barnes and I mopped up the mess. We said lots. He never replied. He didn't even gloat, though I suspect he was mightily pleased by what he had done..

We always tried to avoid these clashes of wills. We wanted the children to see life as a series of choices, of problems that required solutions, rather than battles with winners and losers. To that end, there was only one school rule (other than the one about not going on the roof), which was 'Behave reasonably'. The more rules there were, we thought, the more incentives there were for the children to break one of them. Instead of rules, we made one heavy demand on the children. Whatever went wrong, however badly, they had to talk about it.

On the whole, it worked. They came to accept that we meant no harm, that we weren't trying to get rid of them. I doubt that things are different now, but certainly at that time mainstream schools often grossly underestimated just how frightened some of their problem children were. When Ruby returned to working in a Junior School in the late 1980s, a colleague once described one of the children there as being 'cocky and arrogant'. She asked which child the teacher was referring to. She was astonished when he named a child who had a permanently hunted expression on his face, and bags under his eyes that would have held a week's supply of laundry.

We were at pains to explain that, while we sometimes rejected what the children did, we didn't reject who they were. It was a kind of lay extension of the therapy that Barron practised in his little room at the end of the corridor. None of us believed much in retribution, but we all voted for repair (where possible), repentance (if genuine and appropriate), review (of the day's proceedings, especially the good), reflection, and only occasionally removal. If children gave their group a really bad time, they were placed in another group until they had calmed down. When we didn't let a child go swimming, or on an outing, it was not in the spirit of punishment, but because - as we told them - they were in such a state that they wouldn't enjoy it, and they might turn it into an unhappy experience for themselves and for others.

The outing to the London Transport Museum, then at Clapham, was more of an educational outing, so we didn't have to pretend that it was all about the social development of our children. I remember it for several reasons, none of them anything to do with education. It was the first outing we made to a place where there were pupils from other schools present, a chance, therefore, to see New Riverside children in some sort of educational perspective. On the whole, we didn't do badly. I also remember it because of Micky.

The outing took place on a Wednesday, which was Micky's day for psychotherapy with Barron. I don't want to go into the rights and wrongs of the matter here, because I'm not sure of my ground, but a big factor in my rage on that day was that I didn't think Micky ought to be on the outing - I forget why. I do remember that Micky had been in a simmering fury for several days. On balance, the adults thought that Micky should have to forego the visit. It was better that he had his session with Barron. These sessions were held to be sacred and took precedence over everything else - I seem to recall that Barron had been cross with us for booking a trip on a day when he was in school. I think there was a great deal of unexpressed anger flying about that day. Anyway, to my intense joy, we set off without Micky.

Barron, a wily old bird with that touch of rebellion needed by all who work with maladjusted children, had his session with Micky, and then brought Micky to the Museum in his car. So, after the rest of us had sweated on the bus all the way to the Oval - nearly an hour's journey - and thence had gone by Tube to Clapham, it irked me to see Micky arrive, chauffeur-driven, with that smug smile on his face. The only compensation was that Barron wasn't staying at the Transport Museum. Micky would have to come back with us on public transport.

After touring the Museum, we took the Tube to the Oval, where we joined the queue at the 36 bus stop. It was a long queue, and I doubted that we'd all be able to get on the bus when it eventually arrived. Tom came to the rescue. While queueing, his mind must have wandered to other things, other places. He suddenly came up to me, and cried out in his falsetto: "I'd like to kiss your delicious willie!" I don't know where the thought and the words came from, but they did the trick. The queue dispersed rapidly. The bus came. We all got on.

In July, the finale to the summer term was New Riverside's Official Opening. It was to be a grand affair, with an official photographer, important and powerful friends and enemies from County Hall, from Institutes of Education, from the local community, all in attendance. We had spent the best part of the year praying that the hedge at the front would grow high enough to hide us: now we were to be on public display. We rehearsed songs. We painted pictures. We scrubbed the more legible graffiti off the walls. We tidied the library, removing the books that had the mark of Sally's scissors on them, and putting a brown paper cover on our copy of the Ladybird Famous Figures in History volume on Henry V, which had been re-titled *Henry V IS A CNUT* in big fat permanent-marker letters. It might have been that the intended message was that Henry V was in fact a 'Chut', for 'H's were often written as 'N's. The word 'SNIT' was to be found on walls throughout the school.

Somewhere, there is a photograph of me on the day. I look awful. I have long Seventies style hair, a wimpy little scarf tied loosely at my neck, one of those large-collared shirts, flairs, and Hush Puppies that were going home a bit. But I was smooth and charming in manner, the speeches passed off satisfactorily, and at the end of the day we reckoned we had done ourselves more than justice. That night, we celebrated, and Steve drank us all under the table in the nearby 1930s pub. We had not just survived the first year of the school's existence, we had thrived. We were proud of ourselves.

There was a combined staff and psychiatric team meeting on the last Tuesday of term, when all the children had gone. It was thought that this might be an appropriate time to reconsider in which groups the children were placed. We wrote the name of each child on a separate piece of card, placed them on the table in front of us, and settled down to some horse trading. Ruby put her finger on the card with Micky's name on it, and pushed it as far away as she could.

"Not him," she said. "I'm not having him. Not any more."

She had had enough. The initial report on Micky, that had referred to him as 'stubborn', had been putting it mildly. When Micky wasn't being stubborn, he was patronising to the adults and nauseatingly 'helpful' to the other children, especially Sally. But most of the time he was stubborn.

Micky wasn't right for Steve's group, nor Pete's group. That left mine. Barron thought it would be a wonderful idea if Micky came to me. He remembered Micky's trip to Bournemouth, years ago, in search of his lost father. It was decided that Micky needed a male teacher.

I put a very positive spin on the decision. I was going to rescue Ruby by taking away the child who had made her life a misery, and I was going to fill a most important role in poor little Micky's life. When you asked him how he was, he always said "lil bit happy, lil bit sad". I was going to make him feel a lil bit more happy, and a lil bit less sad. I even felt lil bit more proud of myself.

When it became publicly known that Micky was to move to my group, Barron gave me a piece of advice.

"Never," he said, "*never* get into a confrontation with Micky."

In some ways, it was a silly remark, a bit like saying 'mind you don't get wet in the bath'. Micky lived by, and for, confrontation. It was his best thing. Nevertheless, I made a mental note: I would never get into a confrontation with Micky.

16

Throughout August 1972, a small time-bomb was ticking away in the folder marked 'NEW RIVERSIDE' at County Hall. The local paper reported criticisms from the Inner London Education Authority and the Lewisham Council concerning the length of time it was taking for the school to fill its places. Influential visitors to our Opening Ceremony had noted that here was a school for 50 children that had only half that number on the roll. I still believe that Miriam had been right to be picky as to which children we accepted. There is no point in any school taking on children that it cannot help. But maybe we could have shown a little more urgency.

There was always a backlog of children waiting for placement. Then, as now, there existed a considerable number of children for whom no suitable educational provision was readily available. There were papers on some children that had been doing the rounds for two years or more. Administrators were desperate to place such children, with the result that in some cases special schools were used much as prisons - as a last resort. These children had to be provided with education, which meant they had to be entered on a school role, it didn't matter where. And here was New Riverside, with 25 unfilled places. We were asking for trouble.

But I knew nothing of this when I followed Diana's advice and went to visit Tom at home in mid-August. Diana saw this as a means of building a bridge over the gap in the relationship between Tom and me during the long vacation. She was enthusiastic about the idea. I wasn't.

The visit took place on a boiling hot day, with the sun blazing down as it had for much of that August. I arrived and knocked on the door of the small terraced house where Tom lived with his adoptive mother. There was the sound of rushing feet from inside. The door was flung open. Tom stood there, blinking in the sunshine. His face was pale, and I doubt that he'd had any fresh air or daylight since I'd last seen him at the end of term. Mum appeared behind him.

"This is my mum," said Tom, and his blinking accelerated.

I said 'hallo' and shook her hand.

"Well, go on then," said Tom. "Aren't you going to marry her?"

I was glad when the visit ended. I didn't think I could love Tom's mum for five minutes, let alone forever.

"Don't you want to kiss her?" urged Tom, as we parted on the doorstep.

At the beginning of the September term, we were joined by four new members of staff, one full-time and three part-time. The part-time teachers were Diane East, Mrs Keen, and Ruby's sister Maureen. Let's get Mrs Keen out of the way first because there's very little to be said about her except that she was most inappropriately named. I never discovered her first name, but it couldn't have been Dead. Before becoming a teacher, she had been in the Navy and she came to us straight from Mary Evans's course for Teachers of Slow Learning and Difficult Children. Brian was the full-time member, a home-brew expert and a harbinger of the self-sufficiency craze that was sweeping through the middle class suburbs. There was something of the Workshop Man about him. He had a motorbike and the kind of beard that said: 'This man is good with his hands'. Diane East was a PE specialist, and at last the vaulting horses and the climbing ropes were put to proper use. Diane never had any trouble with the children. At first, the usual knots of spectators gathered in the entrances to the Hall, but as soon as they saw that she knew what she was doing, they decided there would be no messing about. There was no point in watching a professional at work; what brought in the crowds was incompetence. I think that was why my classroom was such a popular venue.

I had already got to know and like Ruby's sister Maureen when her daughter needed somewhere to live while at college and came to board with Sue and me. With the departure of Mrs Askew, we had a part-time teaching vacancy at New Riverside. Maureen was experienced and qualified. Ruby suggested to Miriam that perhaps Maureen could fill this vacancy. Never keen to go through the formalities of convening an interview panel, Miriam had a brief meeting with Maureen, and Maureen was appointed. She signed on to do two days a week as roving Art teacher – though she couldn't use the Art and Craft room as that had been taken over by Brian. Maureen stayed at New Riverside for many years, eventually becoming Acting Head. She was a kindred spirit, deriving laughter and tears from New Riverside in the same proportions and on the same occasions as Ruby and I did.

Joining the staff of New Riverside was not an easy business. Miriam's interviewing technique specialised in making snap decisions. Candidates drove in, parked, stepped out of their cars, and before most of them had taken half a dozen steps, Miriam had made up her mind.

"No. I'm not having him/her. Not in my school." It was a non-negotiable permanent rejection and meant that the candidate would never be paid the slightest attention, let alone an interview. Miriam immediately called the School Secretary to say: "Send him away!... Well, then, think of a reason... Tell him I've had to go out, and tell him not to bother again."

With the ILEA anxious that we should fill our roll, and with the arrival of new staff, we were obliged to take on more children quickly. In the first week of that autumn term, ten new pupils were admitted to New Riverside. It seemed that some kind soul in County Hall had at last appreciated the need to identify and refer maladjusted children early on, for all but one of the ten children were of Junior School age. We re-organised the school to accommodate them. It was decided that Brian should inherit Steve's group, minus Cheryl. I was happy to lose Daryl the Bomber, who went to Pete, and in my innocence I welcomed one of the new children, a lively nine-year-old called Lennie.

Ruby also had two newcomers: Roger, creator of the Sanitary Towel Flying Helmet, and Patrick, who was large for his age (11), and who liked to laugh at any joke, no matter how poor, even if he didn't understand it. Patrick's great love was Amateur Dramatics, where his Ziegfeld-level ambitions always outran both his resources and his patience. He had no time for those who forgot their lines or knocked scenery over. Thwarted when his plans for a *coup de théatre* in one of his most spectacular productions - two giant flying saucers taking off from Ruby's classroom - came to nothing, amateur dramatics turned to amateur histrionics.

We had also decided that we would further develop our plan to make every group a Family Group. So Cheryl stayed with Steve to bring a touch of maturity to a group that otherwise consisted of what we christened 'The Munchkins' - six new boys, all of tender age and only one of a tough disposition. The exceptions to the Family Group system were Brian's group, who were all of secondary age, and my group, who were all Middle School age.

We now had 35 children in the school, roughly seven in each group. Steve had the toughest job, for the Munchkins were a lively lot. I'd never seen Steve lose his temper before, but it quickly became a regular event. I have two mental pictures of him: one of him striding into the Hall, a Munchkin under each arm and two more in his hands - but I think that may be an hallucination - and another of a Munchkin dashing into my classroom and throwing himself under the table.

"Sir's cross," he explained.

This was Matthew. He had had a very troubled life so far, and had only recently left the Maudsley Hospital for a children's home. Matthew's hold on reality was fragile, though he did have those flashes of outsight, the understanding of what others might be feeling. I think Ruby's fondness for him arose while she was pregnant. Matthew was the only person, child or adult, who ever asked her if she was happy that she was going to have a baby. This was many months later, in the summer of 1973. Ruby and I had contacted Matthew's children's home to see if we could take him out for a picnic. I can't remember where we went - it may have been Knole Park, it may have been Keston Ponds - but I do remember Matthew sitting in the back of the car and telling us, *a propos* of nothing at all, that he had once carried the same hanky for a whole year.

Thinking about Matthew has made me realise that however professional and open-minded I tried to be, I instinctively divided the New Riverside children into two groups - the ones I instantly liked, and the ones I instantly didn't like. If I'm honest, forty years later, I have the same likes and dislikes. Though my dislocated finger gives me no trouble, I still don't like Daryl the Bomber. I still have a huge fondness for Leroy, though a few years after he left us, he did some terrible things. Perhaps it's not quite true to say that I still have the same likes and dislikes; it would be more accurate to say I now like or (more rarely) dislike the memory of them. Ruby and I frequently talk about them, and we become tearful when we recall their courage, their spirit, their understanding of each other and of us, no matter how erratically these qualities were applied. And, having written that, I begin to wonder if any of them will come to mind when I'm on my death bed, and which ones.

The other Munchkins were a mixed bunch. There was Jeffrey, whose greatest joy was to be the victim of what he regarded as top class bullying. He was the boy being hit with the unbreakable ruler by Leroy. I once came across Jeffrey writhing on the floor in the Hall, screaming: "Oh, my God, they're murdering me! Oh, help, help! They're killing me!!..." and much more to that effect. But there was nobody else in the room. When I pointed this out to Jeffrey, he rose, scowling, and departed, loudly complaining: "The bastards have all gone!"

There was Simon, who was very quiet, and never did anything wrong in the whole year that he spent with us. We were always waiting for him to do something terrible, or to discover some awful thing he had been doing all the time, but he never did and we never discovered anything. As far as we knew, once he returned to mainstream school, he lived happily ever after. Perhaps some papers had got muddled, and another Simon - a terrible and wretched Simon - had stayed on in mainstream school, giving everyone a bad time.

Wayne was a Munchkin of tough disposition, quick to use his fists and his feet. He lasted less than a term before his physical attacks on other children became too frequent. It's always difficult to absorb violence in any school (or any institution), but many of our children had a history of being violent, and part of our brief was to handle aggression - to an extent, it was what we were set up to deal with. What placed Wayne's continued stay at New Riverside in jeopardy was his apparent lack of any sort of contrition, his reluctance to examine why he did what he did, and the fact that he was a Hostel boy. It was bad enough if any of the children felt the school was not a safe place, but it was worse if any felt unsafe in the Hostel. For five days and four nights a week, the Hostel was their home, and everyone should have the inalienable right to feel safe at home. After three weeks, Miriam refused to keep Wayne at New Riverside. He departed, his papers followed him, and I guess he started the rounds of being accepted by another school, then excluded, waiting for a place elsewhere, being accepted again, and so on and so on… It was a depressingly familiar pattern.

And there was Lennie, who ought to have been a Munchkin, but wasn't because he didn't go to Steve, he came to me . He was small, lithe, and dynamite. His family was notorious. It was said that Peckham Social Services' safe was in their back garden, but no one from Social Services dared call for it. His mother was in prison. His older brothers were in and out of prison. In a way, Lennie wasn't at all maladjusted. He was totally adjusted to his extreme environment. But he was too much for any mainstream school and he wasn't getting any education. Despite what Pink Floyd think, every child both needs and deserves an education, and Lennie was in desperate need of one. He was a tricky lad, but there were times when he made you see life in a different light, and that was sometimes a valuable experience. He was also one of the major players in a little drama that might have ended my teaching career.

17

Mrs Gilbert was a kindly soul, a chain-smoker who rattled along with her cough and stayed in her office, out of the children's way. She may have felt motherly towards me, because my incompetence was poorly disguised, and I always looked a mess. One sunny autumn day she brought me a present - a bottle of home-made blackberry wine, vintage September 1971. As she worked mornings only, she gave me the wine just before she departed at dinner time. I carefully locked it in my stock cupboard - the one in which Tom, Terry and I had had such a memorable darkroom experience back in the early days.

I always took great care to lock this cupboard, to stop children popping into it to break things; or to slash rolls of Sellotape with a craft knife, so that you could never peel off a piece longer than the circumference of the roll; or to use it as a citadel from which to pelt the rest of the group with lumps of Plasticine. But on this day, I reckoned without the skills of little Lennie. Given his family's penchant for mischief and Lennie's own track record, I should have double-checked that, not only was my stock cupboard locked, but that I still had the keys.

My heart sank early in the afternoon, when I heard the cupboard door being unlocked from the *inside*, and turned to see Lennie sweatily emerging, brandishing the keys, that he'd nicked from the pocket of my jacket, which I had stupidly draped over the back of my chair, as though I was somewhere normal.

His eyes blinked in the bright sunshine, he held up the keys as though they were a prize he had won, and he smiled wickedly. "Aha!" he cried. "The keys!" and he bolted out of the classroom. I padded after him, expecting to have to chase him all the way to Peckham, but in the corridor Lennie bumped into Steve, who took the keys from him and gave them to me. I escorted Lennie back to our room, and we all settled down to work.

Time passed. It was quiet. Too quiet. For too long. Something was going on. I did a quick head count. Leroy was missing.

The stock cupboard door again opened from the inside. In my panic, I had forgotten to lock it when I returned with Lennie and the keys. Leroy reeled into the light. He mumbled that he didn't feel very well. There were dark stains on his white shirt, which suggested bubonic plague, but I smelt blackberry. He had climbed on to the top shelf of the cupboard, found this tempting 'bockle', opened it, sampled it, found it sweet and nice, and had swallowed half of it. He was drunk.

He clutched his head and moaned. With a sleight of hand that amazed me, I had the bottle from him and poured what was left of the wine down the sink before anyone else in the room knew what was happening. I explained to the children that Leroy had drunk some juice which had made him ill, summoned Lil Barnes to look after them, and whisked Leroy to the Medical Room. I put him to bed (we didn't bother with *The Three Billy Goats Gruff*), and he went straight to sleep. My worry was that he would still be drunk when the car came from his children's home to collect him - for, as luck would have it, he was going on a special outing after school that day so he wasn't going home on the school bus. We had abrasive relations with children's homes at the best of times.

We felt they were austere, regimented, lacking in humour, well-meaning but boring. They felt we were unstructured (a bit), chaotic (sometimes), and encouraged the children to behave badly (never). It would not do, therefore, to hand over a drunken child who had been entrusted to one's care. Fortunately, Leroy had the constitution of a super-hero, and all signs of inebriation - save the spots on the shirt and a monstrous headache - had disappeared by the time the car arrived.

Though there probably wasn't such a crime as being in charge of a drunken child, once again I feared for my job. Not only did I need the money, I was enjoying working at New Riverside. I was still fathoms out of my depth, but now and then I surfaced and caught a glimpse of what lay beyond the kicking, swearing, spitting, scratching and thumping. I was beginning to understand the signals for help. No child could be genuinely cocky when he or she couldn't read, was loathed at home, and had been kicked out of local school. Few children ever meant it when they said they were 'glad' they had broken something or hurt someone or driven someone away. It was a pathetic attempt to appear to be in control of what they were doing. Most of the children wanted things to go right, but had no idea how to set about it.

Life had been lousy for them. Bad luck had leapt on the back of deprivation, as it so often does. If mum and dad split up, or abandoned them, and Nan became the primary carer, you could bet your life that Nan would die or be taken seriously ill within a painfully short time. If they were fostered or adopted, it was too often by the wrong people for the wrong reasons - "we're going to give you all the things you've never had…this is your home - but don't ever touch the greengage tree in the garden, will you, because my dear father planted that…" Five minutes later, the sound of an axe would be heard, and the dying creak of the greengage tree. If the children were taken into care and looked after by a skilled professional, within a few weeks that skilled professional might well be promoted out of their lives.

But, despite all this - the deaths and separations and abuse and homelessness - they hadn't given up. There was a restless spirit of rebellion within them that urged them not to accept the misery and pain piled on them. They wanted something better. They wanted to be lovable. They went about it entirely the wrong way - making themselves as unappealing as could be, and lashing out at those of us trying to help. But, bit by bit, they began to listen, to talk, to think, to try again. It was what we asked of them, and what they asked of us. They stayed, and tried, and fought with us, and sat on our laps and cried, and let their wretchedness show. It was impossible not to want to stay and see it through.

So I wanted to stay. And I did, for many more exhausting days, weeks, months, years. Mercifully, I don't remember them all, but three days of that term still stick out. One was a day off to attend an ILEA course on Making Musical Instruments. It was a wonderful day. We were shown how to cut wood into frames for home-made xylophones and glockenspiels, and how to cut the metal and wooden bars for the notes. We made maracas and claves, bamboo flutes, and lots of noise, and we were allowed to go to the toilet whenever we liked.

The second memorable day was when I failed to access the mental note I had made, on Barron's advice, never to get into a confrontation with Micky. At the beginning of the term Micky and I passed through what might be called a brief honeymoon period, for it was common practice among the children to want to convince themselves and others that their problems at school stemmed from their previous teacher. If they had a different teacher, all would be well. This tendency was especially strong when children changed teacher at the same school, as it allowed them to display to their previous teacher how much better they were, and life was, with the new teacher. It was as if they were saying to their previous teacher: 'See! See how good and successful I am! Doesn't this prove that all that passed before was *your* fault.'

But the honeymoon came to an end, as all honeymoons do. One sunny afternoon, Micky suckered me into confrontation. It was ten minutes before going-home time. It had been a good day. No broken windows. Nobody hurt. Signs that Leroy might learn to read: "'Yere is... Peter... Yere is... Jane...' Why, Yakky?" There was a pleasant atmosphere, which the children were beginning to accept. Then, for no apparent reason, Micky threw the pieces of a large jigsaw puzzle on to the floor.

"Right," I said. "Pick those up."

"No!" said Micky. He sat down.

"You're not leaving this room until you've picked up every piece of that jigsaw." The moment the words were out of my mouth, little bells rang in my head, and I knew they tolled for me.

"No-o-o!" Micky's voice wobbled as he shook his head. The corners of his mouth pointed at the floor. His face flushed a fighting pink. He folded his arms ominously. Going-home time was not far away. I wanted to go home. Micky didn't. I knew that he didn't, and he knew that I did. And he knew that I knew that he didn't and that there was nothing I could do about it.

But, during my time at New Riverside, I had discovered that if I spoke rapidly, and at length, and without pause, the children could seldom follow the spurious logic of what I was saying. There was just a chance that, if I adopted that technique, Micky might become confused, and that the other children would believe I was having my way, which is sometimes very important for a teacher. It was one of the few weapons in my armoury and I used it sparingly. Micky hadn't come across it yet. I took a very deep breath and began…

"Oh, yes," I said, "that's just what you'd like, isn't it. You'd like me to order you to pick it up and then you'd sit here all night refusing to and all tomorrow and all the day after and the weekend and we'd still be here in fifty years' time waiting for you to pick up the jigsaw well I'm not going to fall for that one I'm not going to give you that satisfaction I'm going to pick up the pieces myself and then it'll be done and you won't be able to just sit there…" And while I was talking, I was on my hands and knees collecting bits of jigsaw and hurling them into the box.

"And now," I said, "that's done" - just like Blind Pew said to Captain Billy Bones when he tipped him the black spot in my favourite scene from *Treasure Island*. I didn't punch the air, but I did make it sound as though I'd triumphed.

Micky and I looked at each other. He was still sitting in his chair with his arms folded. I was standing up and panting hard. We both knew that wasn't how the situation was supposed to have been resolved. We both felt let down, but I think he felt more cheated than I did, and there was nothing he could do about it. After a watchful pause, Micky unfolded his arms, and got up and went home. And so did I.

The third memorable day was that of the outing to Kew Gardens in October. There were to be other awful outings later - notably one to All-Hallows-on-the-Mud when someone popped sweeties into the fuel tank of the ILEA bus, and we had a three hour wait before a replacement bus arrived to pick us up. But Kew remains the worst outing I ever had.

We went on the school bus, driven by Fred. He had a habit of turning respectfully towards you when speaking, so that for maybe fifty metres he wasn't looking where he, or anybody else, was going. Not surprisingly, his driving made the children nervous, which made them hungry, so that they were into their sandwiches before we were out of the school gates. As Brian was ill that day, I had some of his group as well as all mine. With us was dear Mrs Keen. She spoke but once that day, and then unhelpfully.

It started badly. Fred, turning round in the driving seat to speak to me while we were still in sight of the school, clipped the wing mirror of a van parked at the side of the road. The driver shouted. Fred stopped the bus, and wound down his window. I think he was going to apologise, but the van driver wasn't in the mood for 'sorry'. He told Fred what he thought of him, in crude terms. Fred was shocked.

The van driver began to move away, but Fred leaned out of the window and called out. "There's no need for any of that. I went through the war for you."

The van driver spun round, dashed back, grabbed Fred by the lapels, lifted him from the seat, and almost pulled him through the bus window. And while he was doing this, he told Fred a lot more of what he thought of him. When the van driver let go, Fred fell back into his seat. The van driver stomped off. I asked Fred if he was all right.

"Yes, sir, thank you, sir, yes, sir... But he'd no call to do that, in front of the kiddies."

Fred was right. There had been no call for any of that. But the kiddies had so enjoyed the van driver's rich vocabulary that they turned round in their seats to wave and jeer at the van driver as we moved off.

"I think we should go pretty quickly, Fred," I said.

I spent the entire drive to Kew repeatedly telling Fred to look where he was going and trying to appease the children by recounting their favourite fairy stories. My performance was good enough for most of my group, but Brian's sophisticated set (Larry, Jimmy, Charlie) didn't accept the Wicked Witch's motivation in *Rapunzel*, nor the gushing sentimentality of *Cinderella*. They stopped listening and started cheeking Mrs Keen, who preserved a totally bored expression on her face, which disappointed them, and the cheek ceased. Though it pains me to say so, I think it was a victory for the School of Behaviour Modification.

The moment we arrived at Kew, Leroy wrapped his legs and arms round the rail of the school bus and refused to move, muttering that he wanted to go back to Mr Oakes, the superintendent of his children's home. I prised his fingers from the rail, and he unwrapped his legs, and we fell off the bus together and landed in the road. Leroy got up and announced he was walking back to Mr Oakes - a walk that would have taken him at least four hours if he'd had the slightest idea in which direction to head. We wrestled some more, and the Parks Police came along. They were very kind, and said that they thought the problem was that Leroy was probably frightened of the turnstiles. He wasn't, but they were sure he was. They kindly opened the huge ornamental wrought-iron gates, and Leroy and I passed between them, rolling over and over in the dust like fighting dogs, until we were in the park. From then on it was all downhill.

Most of the children disappeared. Leroy stayed with me, wiping away his tears and demanding more fairy stories and more food. We sat on a bench together, where we were joined by Daryl the Bomber (I'm still not sure why he was with us that day), who spent the rest of the day providing a running commentary on all the things that were going wrong. Every few minutes, one or other of the children would rush up, demanding money for food. Having gobbled their sandwiches the moment we left school, they were now hungry. I had been at the game long enough to know that a hungry maladjusted child is a dangerous creature, so I had no choice but to shell out. After a while, Leroy, Daryl and I moved to the café entrance, where it was simpler to press money into every cupped hand that appeared before me.

That was all Leroy and I saw of Kew Gardens that day. After three and a half hours, it was time to head for home.

I had told the children (and Fred, and Mrs Keen) that we were to meet at the bus at ten to two, to give us plenty of time to get back to school.

At a quarter to two we were all there, sitting on the bus, more than ready to go. All save Duggie. We waited… and waited. Two o'clock… five past…

"Right," I said to Fred and Mrs Keen. "Stay here with the children. I'm going to look for Duggie. If I'm not back by twenty past two, you leave."

Mrs Keen, whom I suspected had been sitting in the bus ever since we arrived, said nothing. Fred respectfully argued.

"No, sir. We'll wait here, sir. Don't you worry, sir. Poor little mites." He also kept saying 'thank you', which made me want to hit him.

"You will go at twenty past two."

I left them all sitting on the bus, and did a lap of Kew Gardens, stopping at every gate to give a description of Duggie - searching, hoping, panting. No luck.

On the dot of twenty past two I got back to the bus. It was empty, save for Fred and Mrs Keen. She spoke, for the only time that day. "They've gone," she said, "*all* gone. And I'm glad."

At which moment, Duggie arrived, with a merry smirk on his face.

It wasn't difficult to find the others. Marianne and Anita were having a fight in nearby bushes. Larry and Jimmy were about to be arrested for stealing a stack of Mars Bars from the refreshment kiosk. Micky's wails were coming from the direction of the river. In those days there was no fence separating Kew Gardens from the Thames, and he had climbed down to the water's edge, where he was loudly complaining that he was trapped by the incoming tide. Daryl and Leroy were leaning over the top of the embankment, throwing sticks at him.

I told Micky that he'd better find a way up or he'd drown. I grabbed Leroy and Daryl. With the last of my money, I bribed the refreshment kiosk owner to drop all charges and bribed the children to return to the bus with the Mars Bars that Larry and Jimmy had stolen. In ten minutes we were all back on the bus.

I slammed the door shut and, for the second time that day shouted to Fred: "Drive!"

He crashed through the gears (in random order) and turned round. "Are we in a hurry, sir?" he asked.

I thought of him trying to drive against the clock across the whole of south London. "No," I said. "No, it's all right. Plenty of time."

I flopped into a seat. I was financially broke, exhausted and furious. I felt alone, unloved and exploited. But we were all there, including Duggie, and nobody had been hurt.

And Leroy put his hand in mine. "Tell us a story, Yakky," he said.

"Well," I said, "once upon a time…"

18

It was Miriam's decision that New Riverside's second Christmas should outshine the first, with not only games and food and presents for the children, but also live entertainment. The party food was unnecessary for we had already feasted on our school Christmas dinner. The games produced their usual noisy squabbles. The presents were again sneered at. But the live entertainment showed promise. A strange man entered the Hall, followed by a morose-looking assistant with a gammy leg that made the poor man lurch like Quasimodo. The children fell silent.

The conjuror, a true pro, began by hurling handfuls of toffees into the audience and shouting "Happy Christmas, kids!" The toffees provoked a fresh wave of fighting, but the conjuror's voice rose above the din. "Now!" he shouted. "Who wants to be *tied up*?"

Several wanted to be tied up, for reasons which we shan't go into here. First in the queue was Dennis, a charming boy in Pete's group, who greeted his teacher each morning by saying "Go on, Thomas, hit me… you know you want to". Dennis beamed ecstatically as the conjuror fastened his hands behind his back, but was bitterly disappointed when he discovered the thrust of the act amounted to no more than the display of a series of quick-release knots.

The conjuror threw more toffees, but maybe two o'clock in the afternoon isn't the best time for such sophistication. Though the children remained fearful, their attitude to him and Quasimodo was a supercilious pretence that they were one step ahead of the act all the time. They said they knew

157

exactly what was going to happen, and that they knew how it was done. When the conjuror challenged this, the children were outrageously lucky in their guesses, as maladjusted children so often are. They seem more finely tuned to Fate and Chance than the rest of us, and to have some kind of maladjusted sixth sense. As a result, the conjuror lost much of the confidence on which every illusionist's performance relies. He became confused, to appear not sure what he was supposed to do next. The poor man's bewilderment reached crisis point when he took out a pack of cards, offered the cards to little Sally, and asked her to 'name a card, any card'. Sally blushed with embarrassment, stared at him for a couple of beats, and said: 'Rabbit'. Not having such a card, the conjuror's trick hit the dust. Enough was enough. He hurled the last of the toffees high into the air, to cover a quick exit, and left Quasimodo to wrestle with the children for possession of the props.

Early in the New Year, it was show time once again. The whole school went to see the pantomime at the Whitechapel Art Gallery. This was a matinee performance attended by hundreds of children of all ages, from all sorts of schools. All went well until the halfway stage, when the management of the Gallery boldly threw the interval open to Amateur Talent. Children from the audience were invited on to the stage to sing a song of their choice. Jeffrey leapt up and sang *My Ding-a-Ling*, a performance that managed to be lecherous and boring at the same time, and which was rightly greeted with scorn by the audience. As soon as Jeffrey had been dragged from the stage, up popped our other leading masochist Dennis who took the mike in his hand and gave a virtuoso rendition of Herbie Flowers's *Grandad*, the song made famous by Clive Dunn:

Grandad, grandad, you're lovely,

That's what we all think of you...

It brought the house down and restored the dignity of New Riverside.

At which point, Tom, who had been sitting next to me with his arm linked in mine, and staring more at me than at the stage, began to fidget.

I read the signs and yanked him out of the audience.

"Where are we going?" he asked.

"To the toilets," I said.

"Blimey," he said. "You too?"

The theatre was on the first floor. The Gents was at ground level, across a small yard, at the back of the building.

"There you are," I said to Tom.

"Blimey! I'm not going in there on my own," he said.

"It's all right," I said. "I'll wait for you outside."

"How will I know you haven't gone away?"

"I'll whistle," I said. "You'll hear me."

"It could be anyone whistling," said Tom, with what I realised years later was extraordinary appreciation of potential problems. "I know what - you sing. Then I'll know it's your voice." He turned to go into the Gents.

"Don't you want to know what I'll be singing?" I said.

"Why?"

"In case there's another singer."

"Blimey," he said.

After a short discussion, we settled on *I'll Be Your Long-haired Lover from Liverpool.*

Then Tom went into the Gents and I began singing little Jimmy Osmond's big hit.

All was going well, but Tom always took ages in the loo - I think he found the workings of his body very exciting. I had just reached:

I'll be your clown or your puppet or your April fool...

Cut my hair - I'll even wear a mask…

when three Secondary School lads came down the steps to share a quick lug. It seemed silly to be standing there, by myself, singing:

I'll be your Valentine, and you'll be mine…

at the Gents, as it were, so I stopped singing, and smiled at the lads, to give the impression that all was well, I was cool. I might have got away with it, but a voice of mixed alarm and madness arose from the inside the Gents.

"Why have you stopped singing?"

The sordid little affair that Ruby and I embarked on back in May had become a very serious matter. Ruby and David had separated; Sue and I had separated. I had moved in with Ruby. It seemed that change was in the air that spring and summer. Children left New Riverside. Cheryl's Cuban heels clattered down the corridor for the last time in April. She had been deemed fit to transfer to a secondary school in Croydon. Christina reached school-leaving age in July, departed, and was pregnant before the leaves fell from the trees that autumn – just a few months after Ruby, and quite possibility in emulation of her. New Riverside could no longer countenance the idea of Simon - the Boy Who Never Did Anything Wrong - staying with us. It wasn't that we feared he might become contaminated by staying - maladjustment is not a contagious condition, whatever some educationalists and many politicians might think. It was simply that he had none of the right qualifications. And so, Simon left New Riverside in July, and two months later returned to what our Admissions Register described as "normal school".

Ruby went to Miriam to tell her that she would leave in September, because she was going to have a baby. Miriam and everyone else at New Riverside assumed that David was the father, and Ruby and I didn't tell them they were wrong

- once again I sought sanctuary in being secretive. Miriam may have had mixed feelings about Ruby's departure. She was losing an excellent teacher, but Ruby had been the only adult to stand up to some of Miriam's more extreme outbursts, which both angered and scared Miriam. It was arranged that Ruby would go on working at New Riverside for the first two weeks of the autumn term, to provide continuity for Group 1 while the new teacher moved in.

Steve regularly kept an eye on advertisements in the *Times Ed* and the ILEA's monthly bulletin. He knew that the Inner London Education Authority planned to open five other Day Schools with Hostels for the Maladjusted, and when the next school rolled off the production line, he wanted to be ready to apply for the Headship. Miriam knew all this, and her reaction was to start coaching me to become the next Deputy Head of New Riverside; Miriam was a great believer in the Better-the-Devil-You-Know Theory of Educational Management.

She called me in to her office one morning to make plans for New Riverside's future.

"Next term," she said, "I'm going to do some teaching. I do so miss teaching." There was a pause while both of us tried to believe this. "I want to teach History. I love History. I'll start right now." She picked up the phone, and told Christine, the new School Secretary, to bring a dozen pads, a dozen sets of felt tipped pens, a dozen pens and a dozen rulers. "I'm going to teach History!" she declared down the phone.

Five minutes later, the order was delivered.

"Right," said Miriam. She grabbed a pad and a pen. "History," she said, and she wrote the word firmly in big capital letters at the top of the first page of the pad.

She looked at me. She looked out of the window. We sat in silence.

"No," she said, shaking her head. "I'm bored with that." And she flung the pad on her desk and passed a pleasant half hour listing the faults of the other members of staff.

Towards the end of the summer term, we took some of the children for a week's camping at the ILEA Rural Studies Centre in Haslemere, Surrey. I still don't know why - maybe it was a kind of leaving ordeal for Steve, a last turn of the screw. We took our own tents and our own provisions, and a new arrival (Dave) ensured that we received a special welcome by hurling a raw egg at the Warden of the Centre and spluttering "The yolk's on you", when the egg burst on the Warden's neat new anorak. We spent our days going for long walks to exhaust the children. It didn't work; they always had more energy than we did. I spent my nights in the Stores Tent, guarding the rest of the eggs, and surreptitiously trying to drink beer between unwanted visits from Dennis ("absolutely disgusting things happening in our tent, Yakky") and Tom ("Will you love me forever?"). After the first night, Terry stuck his head in the tent early in the morning, stared at me in horror and said: "God, you look so old!"

At the end of the week, we all went home, and a few days later the second year in the history of New Riverside came to an end.

19

Early in August 1973, Ruby and I were evicted from the flat by her barmy landlord. The reason given for this un-comradely act was that Ruby was pregnant and, in his opinion, this meant she would have a baby and he didn't want a baby in his house. This could have presented Ruby and me and the unborn babe with a tragedy fit for a Hardy novel, and would certainly have made a heart-stopping chapter for these memoirs, but Sue generously moved out of the house in Ladywell, and Ruby and I moved in. I think the neighbours were a little shocked. They had seen me arrive with Sue. They had seen Maureen's teenage daughter join us. And here I was with a third young woman in what was turning into Harem House – all within the space of two years. They may well have been further baffled when Ruby and I went on holiday and the tenor sax player from Battalion moved in.

We camped for a couple of weeks in the mountains of central Wales. The weather was wonderful, the scenery was magnificent, the tent was uncomfortable. Ruby slept a lot, because she was seven months pregnant, and I sat by the river and played the flute because I was going through one of my increasingly frequent bouts of madness.

When we returned to New Riverside in September, Ruby spent the first two weeks of term handing over her group to Cindy, the teacher who was replacing her. It was not an easy job, because Ruby had established strong relations with her group, but it would have been considerably harder if Sally had still been there. For nearly two years I had watched Ruby and Sally explore the World of Infant Education. Sally had come to New Riverside after only a few fiery days at her first school. Ruby had to undo the trauma of that false start and then begin again. It was a delicate task, but one that had those moments of shared joy between teacher and pupil that make it possible for teachers to carry on. The moment I remember best was the day Sally managed to write her first '8'. With cramped little fist and much licking of lips, Sally had already managed to do an 'S'. It took but another minute to force the pen up and round from the tail of the 'S' to turn it into an '8'.

"Done it," she said, pink-faced with pride. "I fink I'll do it ag'in." And she did.

New children arrived - six boys and two girls. Samantha was coolly aware that she was attractive to boys, and pubescent testosterone threatened to inundate the Art Room at the top end of the school. There was no such problem with Irene, who was awkward and not what our lads would have thought attractive in any way. The irony was that the lads formed better relations with Irene, as they didn't have to show off. Samantha held court in the Library, flicking through books (sometimes held upside-down), with a gaggle of courtiers clustered round desperately competing for her attention – much as the male pigeons had been doing for the female pigeons at the Oval, and with about as much luck. Irene, however, could come and go when and where she pleased. No one tried to barge their way into the Girls' Toilet to cheek Irene. Samantha left after just one term, moving with her parents to Scotland. The courtiers were still parading when she departed, at which moment Irene produced one of her prettiest smiles.

The new boys ranged in age from would-be hard-nut teenagers to a five-year-old named Georgie, who wandered about the school like a toddler. One morning, just before school was due to start, I was in the Male Staff Toilets - a couple of wash basins, a couple of urinals, and two cubicles, the doors of which left a gap of about 30 centimetres between their bottom edges and the floor. I was sitting in one of the cubicles, minding and doing my own business, when Georgie's head and shoulders appeared under the door. He squinted up at me, sideways, for there wasn't enough room to twist his body round, and said "You're a naughty boy". He said it with rather more authority in his voice than you might expect from a five-year-old. I didn't argue, even though for once I wasn't being naughty.

Or was I? Was I always? In my father's eyes, I was a naughty boy, and he didn't know the half of what was happening. In October, I took a day off school to be with Ruby for the birth of our son. Miriam approved my absence from work though, as far as New Riverside was concerned, David was the father, not me. Ruby's sister Maureen and their mum knew the truth, but I had kept the whole thing secret from my own family. It wasn't until our son was six months old that I summoned up the courage to tell my brother that he had a new nephew. I had thought he would be shocked, but he wasn't. He was kind and he was reassuring. He told me that all would be well, and it would come as almost a relief to my parents, who at that time feared I had turned into a drug-crazed pimp.

New Riverside had been having catering problems. When the school first opened, we had our team of cooks headed by Mrs Dixon, who was kind and friendly, and a good cook. But Mrs Dixon had been taken away from us back in July - another punishment for not having enough children on the school roll. No longer were school dinners cooked on the premises. They arrived in the back of a van. We were relegated to meals-on-wheels, which meant flabby chips and stringy meat, congealed custard and shrunken dried-out cake, and every dish at the same tepid temperature. The result was that much of the food was rejected and the children went hungry.

We endured the privations of scant rations and poor food bussed in for a couple of terms before our Domestic Bursar had a brilliant idea. Both the school and hostel had large kitchens. Together they could easily cope with providing school dinners for some sixty people. With the approval of the Inner London Education Authority, we cancelled Meals-on-Wheels and went back to self-catering. And we made one other important change. We decided that we would no longer eat as a school in the Hall, but that each group would eat in its own classroom. The food - freshly cooked, piping hot and lots of it - was brought to us on heated trolleys by the hostel ladies. Children chose how much, or how little, they wanted. Each teacher acted as 'mum', doling out beef stew one day, fish pie another, or home-made hamburgers, or shepherd's pie, with all the accompanying vegetables, and then whatever was for pudding - pineapple upside-down cake, rhubarb crumble, rice pudding... And every day, the Domestic Bursar visited each classroom literally seeking feedback from her customers.

We ate well, and we talked between mouthfuls. School dinner became the setting for many conversations of extreme importance. Children saw it as an opportunity to impart news - of visits from their social workers, upsets at home, shattered hopes and new despairs, anything that bothered them. Whereas good news was usually delivered the moment they arrived, bad news was held back until the school family was together at the table. School dinner took longer than originally timetabled, but I don't think any of us ever resented the shortening of our midday break in the staffroom.

There were other signs of progress. Assemblies were no longer interrupted by rooftop protests. There were fewer individual tantrums, and the group tantrum was becoming a thing of the past. Children were slower in responding to gratuitous provocation from their peers. Though never completely silenced, the cry of "I was all right till I came to this fucking dump" was heard less often. Our children were not as scared of life at New Riverside as they had been at their former schools. In mainstream schools, maladjusted children are often very scared, and do things that make them extremely unpopular, with the result that they are often bullied.

A big blow around this time was the departure of Barron. I realised the other day how little I knew about the wisest and most experienced person I ever worked with in twenty-seven years of teaching. After training as a child psychotherapist under Anna Freud, he had worked with delinquent children, with evacuee children in the Second World War, with children in special camps and hostels, and had pioneered much of the work with maladjusted and emotionally disturbed children still practised today. He was the best of teachers, because he knew the truth of what he was preaching. Inspectors and advisory teachers can be sympathetic (or not) and can be seeking to help (or not), but I've only met one inspector who indisputably knew what she was doing (Mary). All the others hoped they were right and thought they were right. That isn't enough. When those working with difficult children are down on their knees (I won't say 'literally', although I did once reach that point) with worry and concern for themselves as well as for the children they teach, they need someone who is strong in his or her beliefs. Barron wasn't always right, no one is, but he was always certain and he was always encouraging, and that was usually enough.

Barron's parting gift to New Riverside was to refer Adam, Luke and Danny to our care. Adam, the smallest of the three, arrived at New Riverside armed to the teeth - toy pistol thrust into the belt on his camouflage trousers, toy knives in each hand, toy grenades stuffed down his pants. Barron was excitedly enthusiastic about Adam's forthcoming placement with us, a partnership he was sure would work. I suppose it must have done to a degree, because the desperado successfully returned to mainstream education six years later. Luke had the curling locks and big eyes of an angel. He was a brave soul, who constructed a life of dreams around the reality of his existence, telling us tales of rich living and luxury at home that we knew weren't true and that he knew we knew weren't true. But they helped him get through the days. We did what we could to help him, but he left two years later. New Riverside could offer him only six-hours-a-day, five-days-a-week. Luke needed more than that, and he moved on to another special school in Kent, that offered 52-weeks-a-year residential education. Danny was the liveliest of the three, and there was something of the 'here we go again' about him. Danny swore, and his swearing went beyond the regular, every day 'fuck off' of the others, further even than Tom's inventive 'fucker-bugger' vocabulary. Danny was a determined lad, with his fists up most of the time. He seldom held on to grudges because, if he felt he'd been wronged, he righted it straightaway, often with a swift kick to the shins of whoever had wronged him. This made him a bit of a problem on the school bus. Madge could have coped with him with liberal use of her 'love taps', but Danny was on Mrs Harrison's bus, and she didn't like him. She complained to Miriam about his behaviour and his language: "Shouting SEE...YOU...EN...TEE... out the window, Mrs Daniels... It's not nice..."

There came an afternoon when Danny's group made trifle in their cooking lesson. Danny hurried out to the school bus, with his trifle, at going-home time, and Mrs Harrison told him to put his trifle on the floor of the bus, between her feet, where it would be safe. He did as she told him. Unfortunately, Mrs Harrison forgot where the trifle was, and when she crossed her legs half way home, she put one of her feet in it.

"Don't matter," she said, wiping bits of sponge and cream and custard off her shoe and smearing them back into the bowl.

But Danny did mind. He wanted revenge. The following afternoon, he and Luke removed the laces from their shoes, fastened them together, and tied the ends to seats on opposite sides of the aisle that ran down the centre of the bus. They then moved to the back of the bus and started a pretend fight. When Mrs Harrison rose from her seat at the front and hurried back to put a stop to the nonsense, she tripped over the shoelaces and fell flat on her face.

Barron was replaced as psychotherapist by Sybil, and the most I can remember about her was that she was big-boned and argumentative. Barron was the toughest of acts to follow, but Sybil should have been in a different circus. She may have been good with children - though I have my doubts - but she was hopeless with adults. She challenged where Barron persuaded, judged where he encouraged, and trod the narrowest of paths whereas Barron roamed freely. Unlike Barron, who was only too happy to enter the lions' cage, Sybil stayed well outside the big top. Sybil didn't last long. She was succeeded by a bloke, too insipid to warrant criticism.

Comings and goings continued throughout the autumn of 1973. The uneasy partnership that Ellen and Tammy had forged at New Riverside was broken when they left to go to different schools. I was sorry to see them go. Each possessed a tight-lipped sense of humour. A tiny smile used to appear on poor, fragile Ellen's weary face, indicating that she had caught a glimpse of how comically ridiculous life could be, which must have made a change from the norm of 'grim'. There had been one glorious cookery session when Ellen had so exasperated Mrs Keen that the ex-Wren slammed a mixing bowl down on the work surface and shouted: "I'm not your fucking slave!" And there was one morning when Ellen found life so upsetting she shut herself in the loos at her children's home and would only agree to coming out if Miriam came and drove her to school. I don't know what prompted this. Some people might well see it as manipulation on Ellen's part, but they'd be wrong, as people often are when they attribute bad motives to 'bad' behaviour in children.

The catch phrase of Tammy and Ellen's double act was 'shit and sugar'. It was their stock response to almost any question that could be answered by using nouns only. "What shall we cook today?" "Shit and sugar!" What would you like for Christmas?" "Shit and sugar!" "What's blocking the sink (yet again)?" "Shit and sugar!" "What rhymes with 'doctor'?" "Shit and sugar!" Their basic *schtick* was to race through any task they were presented with and then demand another. They knew I couldn't keep up with them, and this failure on my part justified the criticisms they heaped on me: "Call yourself a teacher...", "How am I supposed to learn if you don't give me any work...", etc. And yet, I really was sorry to see them go.

I had no such feelings of sorrow when Terry and I parted and he went to Steve's group. Terry still believed all his troubles would be ended there, with the big boys. That didn't happen, but Miriam decided that he had made enough progress to transfer to a local secondary school at the beginning of 1974.

I had also lost Tom, who had gone to join Pete's group. He must finally have let go of my arm in the summer of 1973, but I don't know exactly when. You seldom notice these 'last times' in life - the last time you read a bedtime story to one of your children, change a nappy, cut up their food, help them get dressed, remind them to take their PE kit to school... But we all know when we last held the saddle and ran alongside them on the day they learned to ride a two-wheeler. I don't even know the last time Tom asked me if I would love him forever.

With a new baby and a host of friends repeatedly asking when we were going to have another, it was time to run away again. We left London and bought a late 19th century terrace cottage near a village on the Kent and Sussex border. The village was inhabited by two classes – the wealthy, who commuted to London each weekday, and the peasantry, who were kettled on a council estate. It was here that, at long last, I had the courage of my long-held convictions and joined the Communist Party of Great Britain – just in time to see it dismembered by its own leadership.

I commuted to New Riverside by car, a daily round trip of some 50 miles, which meant leaving before eight in the morning and returning after six in the evening. We sold the Mini-Traveller and the A35 van and replaced them with an ancient rusty-but-plucky Morris Minor (which cost £60 and gave us three years of totally trouble-free motoring until the day we returned to London in 1978, when it died on arrival), and a large and unreliable Morris Oxford Estate. The latter was Ruby's only means of escape. Even in the 1970s it was impossible to live in the country without a car; the nearest bus route was more than a mile away, and the bus service was infrequent. There was a little shop run by a small racist in the village, but walking there with a push-chair was impossible.

The nearest pavement was miles away, the footpaths were usually ploughed up, and there was barbed wire everywhere. The villagers didn't like us because we were scruffy and mildly hippy and were known to read the *Morning Star* - I think the newsagent in the nearby town snitched on us. The more Ruby and I showed our real selves, the wider the gulf that opened between us and the rest of the village population.

Back at New Riverside, life wasn't the same without Ruby. I missed her. I missed the intensity of our professional relationship. Though surrounded by children, teachers live solitary working lives. The adult company they get at work is only available during short breaks in the staff room, where colleagues chat about television, the special offers in Argos and IKEA catalogues, and John Lewis fabrics. Admittedly, life was different at New Riverside, where teachers were compelled to come together because happenings tended to spill out of one room and involve the inhabitants of others. But Ruby and I had worked intimately together, forming theories and principles relating to the education of problem children, theories in which we had sufficient confidence to hold inviolable. I don't know about the sum being more than the parts, I'm certain my part was less when Ruby wasn't there and there wasn't a sum.

New Riverside was still growing. In the calendar years 1973 and 1974, we admitted 21 boys and 5 girls. Samantha, Irene, Polly (who was like Cheryl in a good mood), and Beth (who liked to chat to the adults over cups of tea) were all teenagers. Years later, Beth wrote to Maureen describing life after school as 'If it is not one thing, it is another'. The fifth girl was tiny Lynette, who received the gentlest treatment of any child at New Riverside. She was quiet and sweet, and gave the lie to the belief that, though fewer girls made it to maladjusted school, those that did were far harder to manage than any boys.

The 21 boys were a mixed lot. They contained the oldest maladjusted pupil that I ever came across, the most dynamic, the most mild-mannered, the two most boring, and two brothers named Joel and Max. The brothers lived on a vast campus of children's homes near Sidcup, founded by the Poor Law Union of Deptford and Greenford in 1902. There were twenty inappropriately named 'cottages', with fifteen girls aged from four to sixteen in each, and five 'blocks' for the boys. The campus was a gloomy place, and Auntie Gwen and Auntie Ivy, who ran the brothers' cottage, were gloomy people. Max and Joel's mother had disappeared from their lives, and the maternal role had been taken by Grandma, a formidable woman, smartly dressed and tastefully blinged, who never tired of telling us that her brother was a successful lawyer in Sweden. I suspect that she was a frequent visitor to Max and Joel's blockhouse, for Grandma had much to say about the shortcomings of the place and of Auntie Gwen and Auntie Ivy, though her criticisms were made in language so beautifully phrased that the Aunties might have had difficulty in understanding it.

Early in 1974, Steve left to take on the headship of a cloned version of New Riverside School and Hostel near London Bridge. I had been thoroughly groomed to step into his shoes, and it was reckoned that the outcome of the interview for the job was a foregone conclusion.

"Do remember to dress *nicely* for the interview," said Diana, smiling such a big smile at me that it almost disguised her fear that I might turn up in the absurd flower-power gear I'd worn for the Official Opening. I didn't repeat that mistake. For the interview, I dressed suitably and went back to pretending. It probably helped that Miriam allowed the

School Governors little choice as to who was to be appointed, for she knew I would give little trouble. Whatever the reason, the job was mine.

Teachers came and went. Sometimes, they left of their own accord, sometimes they were pushed. Mr Everett was earnest and weak, but arrived with the label EX HEAD TEACHER attached to his name. We made the mistake of assuming that he would therefore perform well. He didn't. Breaking point was reached on the day he brought his prized belonging to school, just as Mrs Askew had so rashly brought her box of beads. It was a machine that polished stones. I have no idea why he brought it to school - toys weren't allowed. Nor do I have any idea how the stone-polishing machine worked. I only know that it didn't work for very long once it reached New Riverside, and that Mr Everett departed a week later.

He was followed by Mrs Saltmarsh, also earnest and experienced, and a brave soul, but you could see her ears wince when assailed by the children's frequent use of not-nice words. Nevertheless, she soldiered on until the mess rather than the language proved too much for her. After Mrs Saltmarsh came Don Barnett, a young physically-handicapped American teacher. Mr Ackroyd, our new school inspector and successor to Dr Snooper, thought it would be an excellent idea if New Riverside employed Don, explaining that the example of Don's overcoming the loss of an arm would prove an inspiration to our children.

In giving this explanation, Inspector Akroyd revealed that he didn't know what he was talking about. He hadn't the slightest notion as to how maladjusted children's minds work. He believed they had the ability and will to place themselves in the shoes or minds of others. Thus, they would be able to rid themselves of some of their own maladjustment by observing the excellent re-adjustment that Don had made.

But the only effect that Don's handicap had on our children was to frighten them. Don had only one arm. In their eyes, that was scary. On top of that, an air of mystery hung about him.

Because he was a young American male, and his father was a high-ranking officer in the US Army, and he spoke about lying in a hospital bed next to Vietnam vets, we had made our own assumption - that Don had been severely wounded in the Vietnam war, which had ended about three years previously. It came as Surprise Numbers 1 and 2 to learn that Don had never been to Vietnam, and that he had lost his arm in the US following a motorbike accident. It was his right arm that Don had lost, and I thought his appalling handwriting was because he'd had to learn how to write all over again with his left hand, so it came as Surprise Number 3 to learn that he was naturally left-handed. It came as no surprise to learn that he was in a deep depression, a state that most maladjusted children instinctively recognise, and which may be every bit as upsetting to them as a physical handicap.

Surprise Number 4 was the way they reacted to this. As Deputy Head, I was free to dine in any classroom. Most of the time I kept to a regular schedule - Mondays with Group 1, Tuesdays with Group 2, and so on. Only if there was an emergency did I depart from the timetable and, lest there be any doubt, I moved towards the emergency, not away from it. When I first ate with Don and his group, I discovered that all the children were using only their left hands to eat, holding their right arms limp by their sides. They were not conscious of this, it was simply an instinctive mirroring of what Don was doing. Don didn't last long. As his depression began to lift, a great deal of anger within him rose to the surface, sometimes reaching the point of physical violence. I don't think the children ever hit back.

We did our best for Don, in and out of school. Maureen gave him a lift to school each day. Many Tuesday meetings were devoted to him. He had frequent sessions with the big-boned psychotherapist – these were the only times I felt truly sorry for him. My own contribution was to pretend that I was happy to give up a Saturday to remove old nails from the floorboards of the sitting room in his Clapham flat, in preparation for the floor being sanded. I can still smell the choking fumes from the coke-burning stove, mingled with the dust from the floor, and I can still hear Don's depressed voice, pointing out nails I had missed as I crawled over the floor, collecting splinters in my hands and knees.

"There's another you missed… right there… and another, behind you… And two more over there, in the corner… This is taking for ever…"

My reward for helping him was a week's painful chest infection, and in all honesty I wasn't sorry when Don became another of the select set of teachers who were encouraged to go.

Some of what I thought at the time, and maybe much of what I have recorded here, is unkind. There is nothing inferior in a teacher who cannot work successfully in a maladjusted school, nor is there anything necessarily superior in one who can; just as playwrights aren't inferior or superior to novelists. We all go through life seeking where and with whom we can be at our most competent, and there are bound to be disappointments along the way. What we had to call into question were the reasons why some teachers had opted to teach in a maladjusted school. I'm not sure what would constitute a good or valid reason, but it became clear at New Riverside that a sense of missionary zeal wasn't one. Nor was feeling a personal need to work in what they hoped was a therapeutic community. Nor was the conscious or subconscious feeling that they were heading for a nervous breakdown, and would thus understand just how the children felt. And nor was a vague feeling that they'd like to discover more about themselves.

Each time a teacher departed prematurely, I found myself again a group teacher, plugging the gap they'd left, which was how I became embroiled with Monty... or, rather, Mon'y.

Despite his huge blue eyes and his long eyelashes, there was a dodgy look about Monty, as though he was about to do something he shouldn't do, and that you knew this was so, and that he knew you knew. He would clumsily set out to nick a pen or too much food or a copy of one of the *Ladybird Well Loved Tales*, but would immediately put whatever it was back where it belonged, looking you straight in the eyes and saying "no, 's all right ... go on with what you were saying...". His major weakness was that he was bereft of all social skills; his greatest strength was that he believed exactly the opposite.

In April 1974, going through another bout of extreme madness, I took some of our children to the Oval, to watch the first day of Surrey versus Derbyshire. It was a miserable game, on a bitterly cold day, with frequent rain-filled interruptions. During one of these, Monty announced that he was going for a walk. He waved his arm to take in the entire Oval.

"If I walk all the way round," he said, "will I get back here?"

Part of the purpose of these expeditions was to give children practice at managing on their own, in new settings. The Oval was a clearly defined location with a walled circumference, and I figured Monty was most unlikely to get lost. It might at a stretch be considered an educational experience for Monty to learn this property of all shapes with a circumference or parameter. To be honest, I also figured that ten minutes without him would be no bad thing, so I told him that he would certainly come back to where he started.

He was a long time gone. When he came back, red in the face, he asked me if I was all right. I said I was, and asked him if he was all right. He said he was, but slipped off his blue anorak and stuffed it out of sight under his seat, looking over his shoulder as he did so, as though expecting company. The steward who arrived half a minute after Monty was a man in his sixties, probably with high blood pressure. He was out of breath, in a rage, and very much redder in the face than Monty. He looked at the children. Then he looked at me. I said nothing, and I tried to put a look on my face that suggested we were a party from a fee-paying school. Although there were only about three dozen spectators at the Oval that day, the steward couldn't be sure that one of us was the cause of his fury, so he issued a general threat.

"If I ever catch any of you here again," he panted, and I realised that 'any' included me, "I'll make every one of you wish you'd stayed at home."

We all kept very quiet, and Monty spent the rest of the soggy afternoon trying to make friends with a pigeon.

"Look, Yakky," he said. "He likes me."

As far as I could judge, few creatures great or small liked Monty. I didn't want to bring this to his attention, and it would have been cruel to point out that pigeons are not only vermin, but have lousy little brains that are incapable of liking anybody. I just kept my mouth shut. Happily, the rain increased to the point where cricket was ruled out for the day and we could all go back to school.

During these times when I was called upon to be a stop-gap Group teacher, I fell back on my old, worn-out practices. The pre-morning break quiz was revived, and pirates once more put to sea in their square cardboard galleons and sailed across paper oceans to Treasure Island. Monty rapidly became my favourite buccaneer, because his quiz answers always caught me on the starboard bow when I had expected a portside engagement. On one occasion I had asked another pirate to name three of the planets (this was only a few years after the Moon landing and the launch of the Mars space probe, so Space had a high profile). We'd got as far as 'Mars' and 'Saturn', but there we had stuck, until Monty leaned forward excitedly and said: 'What about Vagina!'

Monty's ambition to excel in a quiz situation led to leaps of the imagination, almost frightening with their audacity. On one occasion I explained to my group that humans and other creatures were divided into two types, called 'carnivores' and 'herbivores'.

"Now," I said, "one type eats meat. Which one do you think that is? "

There was a moment's silence, then the glow of virtue and knowledge appeared on Monty's face. Here at last was a question he could answer.

"Lesbians," he said.

After that I gave up the daily Treasure Hunt. I thought it had peaked.

But my most abiding memory of Monty is of an exchange that took place in the late autumn of 1975, on a Wednesday afternoon. I was shepherding a small flock of New Riverside's middle-aged pupils, on the way back from the recreation ground where we had spent the afternoon playing football. It was about ten minutes before going-home-time and we had just reached the school gates. As we shuffled in, one of the older lads came storming out of the school. His name was Ralph, and he was then about fifteen years old. He was big, muscular, highly volatile by nature, and someone who gave off the most terrifying vibes of wrath. As Ralph charged through the flock, scattering it in several directions, Monty raised his hand in greeting and cheerily said to him: "All righ', Ralphie?"

Without even slowing down, Ralph snapped back: "Fuck off, you little cunt!"

Monty turned to me. "He's my best mate," he said.

20

We had become a real school. We had the requisite number of children on the roll. We had five functioning family groups. We had (very occasional) football matches against other schools. We had our specialist PE teacher, and two part-time specialist Art teachers (Ruby and Maureen). We even had a Careers Officer, who officially came once a term to the school, but who was prepared to put in unpaid overtime for our children. His name was Nigel Barker, and he was a member of the congregation of Miriam's church ('church' here meaning 'building' - as far as I know, Miriam hadn't started her own religion). Nigel was a quiet, pleasant man, whose job was not easy. The national unemployment rate rose steadily throughout the mid-1970s, from roughly 3.5% to 5.8%; not exceptionally high by today's lousy standards, but not helpful to New Riverside school leavers who were perhaps the least likely contenders for any jobs available. They had no educational qualifications, few had mates already in employment who could help them from the inside, and even fewer possessed mastery of the interview technique.

As well as being a pleasant bloke, Nigel was honest. He told us that he could always find a job for any of our children at the paper bag factory in New Cross. The factory always needed workers, for the simple reason that no one could stand working in it for more than a week. The noise made by the machines was deafening. The factory was broiling hot in summer and freezing cold in winter. The opportunities for promotion were non-existent, unless you count making a bigger paper bag as climbing a rung up the admittedly very short career ladder to the top of the Paper Bag Business. So, though he may well have been tempted to, Nigel didn't recommend the manufacture of paper bags as a promising career for any of our children. It made his job much harder but he slept better at nights with a clear conscience.

I don't know how, but Nigel found work for almost all our school leavers and some did well. Kenny (he of the gifted right hand - smoking, V signing, and nose-picking simultaneously) started working life as a shelf-stacker at a branch of a leading supermarket chain, and within a short time had risen to Manager of the Wines and Spirits department of one of their London stores. In this, as in much of his development, Kenny received tremendous support from one of the staff at his children's home. I suppose life is always a lottery in terms of the adults that Fate decrees shall look after us - parents, teachers, guardians, foster-parents, and child care staff - the very stuff from which fairy tales and the plots of most of the novels of Dickens are made.

In an attempt to provide some of our children with educational qualifications, we considered the pros and cons of entering some of the older children for CSE exams, which were the immediate forerunners of GCSE. The pros were obvious if the children succeeded; the cons were just as obvious if they failed. To enter the children for exams would be to take a gamble with their fragile self-esteems. The reason why we were having this debate was that we had eight 14- or 15-year-olds of rare potential - they were certainly intelligent enough, and they seemed to have the necessary application. This gifted sub-group consisted of two girls and six boys, and they came together every day from different groups in the school for lessons in Art, English and Maths. We bought textbooks and followed the exam syllabus, and these sessions were the happiest teaching times I ever had. And the proudest moment in my on-the-whole sorry career was the day in 1977 when Mary Evans entered the Hall at New Riverside, and there we were, at our tables with our graph paper, compasses, protractors, and our well-sharp pencils doing our Geometry with not a fag end in sight.

The two girls in the group were Sandra and Jayne. They were not natural buddies, but girls were always thrown together in New Riverside, because of their scarcity. Out of the first 240 children admitted to New Riverside, only 39 were girls. Sandra and Jayne arrived at New Riverside within six weeks of each other in the spring of 1975, and had no choice but to hang around together. They appeared happy enough much of the time, but at heart there was a heavy sadness in both of them.

Alec and Raymond were both in the Hostel, were very much mates, and were less obviously sad. Raymond in particular had an almost permanent air of amused contentment. There was something of the cocktail party guest about him, as though he was happy to indulge in small talk, about the state of the Market, the weather, how to find a decent tailor. Alec was more argumentative, though seldom to the point of confrontation – he quite rightly saved that for the Hostel. Children in the Hostel were expected to reveal their problems in that setting, rather than in the school. If the school was run on psycho-dynamic lines, the hostel went further, functioning as a therapeutic community. Life was supposed to be different for the day children, who were expected to show their disturbance at school rather than at home, where their parents or foster-parents or children's home staff might have struggled to understand what was going on.

We were warned against the dangers of seeing ourselves as a 'therapeutic community'. Did we know what that meant? Did we know how it should be run? Were we using the word 'therapeutic' pretentiously? In the 1970s, there was much talk in psychiatric educational circles about such institutions as the Mulberry Bush and the Cotswold Community (where Barron had worked as visiting psychotherapist). We were not in the same league. The Cotswold Community had no half terms or holidays or even weekends. The provision was open 52 weeks in the year, 7 days a week, 24 hours a day. We could not work with the same intensity, that wasn't really our function. Our brief was to help the children to the point where they could realistically return to mainstream school, and could manage the problems of life within their own families and communities. There were times when we were in danger of stumbling across the line between school and therapeutic community but, on the whole we successfully kept to our brief.

In addition to Sandra and Jayne, Alec and Raymond, the CSE group consisted of Ian, Bernie and Ross, all of whom faced life by locking problems away inside them, rather than by throwing tantrums or starting fights. Bernie was very quiet and very smiley, and a genuinely nice lad. Ross looked as though everything in life was a great worry and too difficult for him to manage, but somehow he did enough to get by. Ian was quiet, highly intelligent, and I couldn't help thinking that he must be with us under false pretences.

After just one day in a secondary school, he had become a school-refuser. Some might see this as an extreme reaction, but school is the only compulsory institution in our society. We all have to go there, whatever we have done or not done. It's not like prison or hospital or anywhere else, and it doesn't suit every child. After Ian had had a good look at New Riverside, he paid us the silent compliment of not turning us down. Most of all, Ian wanted to know about Art and Music - though not necessarily *Leaving on a Jet Plane* or *Feelin' Groovy*, both of which I'd done to death by the time he joined us in 1975. He wanted to learn how to play classical guitar, not the chord-strumming rubbish that I dealt in. Ruby had studied at the Spanish Guitar Centre in London, so she gave him lessons. Ian was a fast learner, and within a term, Ruby reckoned he had consumed all she knew. Strangely, the day after I wrote the previous few sentences, I received an email from Ian. I had had no news of him since he left New Riverside in July 1977, but here he was, almost thirty-four years later. The email said he was well, still playing the guitar, and earning his living as an artist.

And then there was Trevor, from the same children's home as my beloved Leroy. Trevor nearly qualifies for a book of his own. Like Leroy, I don't think he had any memories of his father. He had a brother who was not in care, and he had intermittent contact with his mum. There was a sadness hanging about Trevor, but occasionally a kind of joining-in jollity would emerge, when he was playing football on the playground. He knew he wasn't a skilled player, being naturally clumsy - objects broke in his hands, slipped through his fingers, overturned in his grasp - but he turned this into a kind of joke, as though he was taking the piss out of his own poor physical co-ordination.

As Warden, Miriam had a small house attached to the Hostel. She lived there during the week, spending the weekends at her own flat a couple of miles away. Once the Special Sub-Group was well established, Miriam decided that they should spend a week separated from the rest of the school, mornings only, to meet together in her house. It was to be an extension of their social education, a chance to discuss philosophy, current affairs, and the children's future careers. I was instructed to join the party.

We gathered together for the first time in Miriam's sitting room one Monday morning. Miriam had arranged that the week should start with a tea-and-coffee welcome session. I'm not sure why. We all knew each other extremely well, and we never started the day together with what amounted to compulsory light refreshments. For Trevor, it was a foreseeable bad start. He put too much sugar in his cup, stirred it too briskly, lost control, and cup, saucer and contents ended up on Miriam's light-coloured carpet. Trevor was horribly embarrassed. "Oh, sorry, sorry, sorry," he said, over and over again. It was his catchphrase. I think he felt he had failed some kind of test, and perhaps he had.

I have no statistical evidence to support this theory, but I think there is a direct correlation between clumsiness and lack of self-esteem. For most of our children, few encounters in life were free from any anxiety. So much that they did was done awkwardly, with hesitation, without confidence. That was obvious from their body-language. And this had a clear knock-on effect in all that they did. They could rarely devote themselves to the task in hand, and this was particularly true of unfamiliar tasks, or tasks performed in unfamiliar situations or in front of strangers. It is impossible to concentrate when the mind is full of doubt and worry, about home, parents, failing to please, failing to read, dangers in the street, and a great deal more.

The post of Deputy Warden of the hostel now fell vacant, and as there were no applicants for the post - or so Miriam said – it was suggested that I should serve as stopgap for a term or two, combining the job with being Deputy Head of the school. I would receive a small allowance, and I could move with Ruby and our son into the little two-bed maisonette that went with the job. This was more or less essential, for we only had one car, and without another for Ruby in the country, life for her and our son would have been impossible. Miriam repeated that she thought it might be good for the Hostel children to see that Ruby and I were prepared to entrust our own son to the care of New Riverside. Whether she really thought that, or whether it was simply a ruse, I have no idea.

We became weekly commuters. On Monday mornings, we packed our bags, grabbed the cat and set off for suburbia. On Friday afternoons, we packed our bags, grabbed the cat and set off for our country retreat. I slept in the hostel one night a week, as Staff Duty Member. The working hours of the extended day (i.e. those before breakfast and after school) were tiring, and I sometimes had little energy left after reading bedtime stories to the younger hostel children and after having late night discussions with Alec and Raymond about the Meaning of Life and the Practice of Sex (which doesn't seem to make Perfect). The extra money that I received as Deputy Warden was welcome and would have been useful if Ruby and I hadn't spent the bulk of it on gin to comfort us at this time of added stress.

One lasting image of the eight weeks or so that we spent in the hostel concerns a twelve-year-old boy named Miles. In school, Miles presented himself as cocky, un-cooperative and a nuisance. He was hard to like. In the hostel, he was much the same, or so I thought, until my first night on patrol, when I went into his room and saw him tucked up in his bed, sleeping deeply. He looked like the Dormouse in A A Milne's poem, for I found 'that he lies fast asleep on his front with his paws to his eyes...' That image made me change my mind about Miles and I never again regarded him as cocky - though he was still un-cooperative and a blooming nuisance.

21

As Deputy Head I was occasionally sent in Miriam's place to the Banding Meetings. I was initially nervous, but soon became irritated instead. The meetings were slow in coming to business. There would be tea and biscuits and chat. It took ages for the meeting to get under way. The other two heads were Steve (my predecessor as Deputy Head at New Riverside) and Mrs O'Reilly, who was Head of an older ILEA maladjusted school in a neighbouring borough. Mrs O'Reilly was an alcoholic legend in her lifetime. The first time a Department of Education inspector paid her an unexpected visit, she was able to convince him that the gin bottle on her desk was a paper-weight. The second time, when his visit had been announced in advance, her persuasive powers failed her.

In these Banding Meetings, she was always two or three sets of papers behind those that the rest of us were discussing.

"Little Susan, now…"

"We've finished talking about little Susan, Mrs O'Reilly. We're on to Leonard Filkins."

"Leonard Filkins? I don't have any papers about him…"

"They're on the floor by your feet…"

"Let me see…"

And there would be a pause in proceedings while Mrs O'Reilly searched through the many sets of papers that she had dropped on the floor.

"Let me see, now… What was that name?…"

One hot afternoon we were discussing a ten-year-old boy, one of whose symptoms was that he regularly soiled himself.

A certain reluctance to take him hung in the air, as might be expected on a hot afternoon.

"Ah, what problem is there in a little thing like soiling?" said Mrs O'Reilly. "You just get him to take off his pants, give them a little rinse through, then a little wash… I've done it dozens of times for little ones. How old is he? Ten years old! That's still young. He can come to my school…"

"You're sure?"

"Sure I'm sure."

"OK. We'll put him down for your school."

"Of course. That'll be fine." And then Mrs O'Reilly's voice suddenly changed as she added: "Let him soil his pants in my school, if he dare."

We usually had a soiler or two at New Riverside. Our then current champion was Peter, a bulky 13-year-old, referred for special education by Lewisham Health Authority. Peter was a lethargic and unhappy lad who oscillated between unconvincing matey-ness and foul-mouthed rage. It was hard to like him, but my feelings towards him changed considerably after I attended a meeting with his mother and father. Mother was aware of Peter's soiling problem, but was highly critical of the school's failure put an end to it.

"I know my Pete does this," she said. "The trouble I've had. Sometimes you have to cut up his doings with a pair of scissors… Peter's like his father here…" She indicated Peter's father, a small man who was hiding in the corner of Miriam's office. "*He* used to be a chronic bed-wetter, until we got married. I soon put a stop to that." From then on my sympathies were with Peter.

I also attended the initial interview that Miriam conducted with each family before the child was admitted to school. Some of these interviews were sad and moving, some were full of hope, several gave glimpses of life and issues to come.

When Mr and Mrs Bolton brought their son Jeremy to the school, Mr Bolton was finding it impossible to understand why Jeremy had been excluded from the local secondary schools.

Miriam was at her best on such occasions, asking direct questions, and blowing away the smokescreens that some parents wished to create.

"What reason did the school give?" she asked.

"Well," said Mr Bolton. "They said that Jeremy had smashed a whole row of wash basins. Now, why on earth would he do that?"

Jeremy agreed, echoing the words and voice of his dad. "Why on earth would I do that?"

We never found out why. Nor did we find out why, a couple of months later, Jeremy took a hammer to the school's six typewriters.

New pupils continued to arrive. Jennifer was an ungainly eight-year-old, who used to sidle awkwardly along the school corridor, muttering what sounded worryingly like curses. There was a day when I was showing a visitor round the school. I forget the name of the visitor, but she was a dental hygienist who was preparing the way for her forthcoming second visit when she would examine the children's teeth. I was taking her from class to class, introducing her so that the children would know exactly who she was and why she had come, hoping that they wouldn't be frightened when she returned for the dental examinations.

We came across Jennifer, body pressed against the wall, head hidden from view behind a fire extinguisher.

"Hallo, Jennifer," I said. "This lady is going to come and tell us how to look after our teeth."

Jennifer somehow coiled herself round the extinguisher. "Fucking witch," she said, and sped up the corridor like a spider falling over its own legs.

Jennifer's boyfriend was seven-year-old Jonathan - there was talk of their getting married, but nothing came of it - yet another unhappy child, who saw the world and its entire population (except Jennifer) as at best darkly threatening, at worst outrageously cruel. This led him to desert his own classroom frequently and to barge into any of the other rooms. On entry, he would slam the door behind him, stand to attention, shaking with rage and, with tears in his eyes, bellow: "There's far too much noise in this room! You're all in detention!" I don't recall any of the children giving Jonathan a bad time as a response to his bizarre behaviour.

Among the newcomers was Sean, a nervously excited lad who was into punk. He wore studs in his ears, and sometimes came to school with streaks of puce or lime green in his fair hair. During one cooking session in the Home Economics Room, he sprinkled artificial colouring in his cake mix. When the cakes were baked, he proudly showed them to his teacher. "Look, Miss," he said, "punk rock cakes."

Unfortunately, Punk Sean's teacher (let us call her Julie) preferred worry to laughter, and didn't appreciate the joke. Julie carried a perpetual frown on her forehead, because she was worried about the Spectre of Sex. The children in her group quickly picked this up, using the same radar system that had almost been the undoing of Ruby and me in the days of our sordid little affair. They seemed to play on Julie's 'thing' about sex, drawing inaccurate pictures of it, asking ridiculous questions about it, and talking endlessly about it.

"It's just been sex, sex, sex in here all morning," was Julie's frequent complaint.

She knew that Talking was the school's currency, so several times a week she sent for Miriam (or more rarely for me) to come to her room as she wished to have a group talk about some problem or other. They were usually not very big problems, even when sex was allegedly involved. The trouble was Julie was profligate in her use of Talking. The whole business of Talking was being devalued. Sean saw what was happening long before Julie did. He never directly pointed this out to her, but as soon as anything went wrong in her room he would close his books, put them in a pile, place his pen neatly by the side, fold his arms and say: "All right, then, let's have a talk, let's have a boring talk…".

Anthony first arrived at New Riverside in a chauffeur-driven limousine one February morning in 1975. To be honest, it wasn't really a limo, it was a Ford Cortina, and the chauffeur was really a houseparent from yet another children's home in Croydon. But there was a touch of class about Anthony – he had the *insouciance* of Noel Coward and the voice of Wilfrid Hyde-White. That first morning, Anthony arrived in grey flannels and a double-breasted navy blue blazer with a lavishly decorative badge on the breast pocket. Also - unless my imagination has wrestled memory to the ground – he occasionally flourished a large coloured handkerchief. Smiling broadly, and looking brimful of confidence, Anthony saluted Miriam, who was inspecting him from her office window.

He was eleven years old, had been in care most of his life, but still hoping that somehow, somewhere, sometime he would see his mum again. Until that day came along, he had his houseparent (whom he called 'Uncle') and his social worker ('Harry'), and for four and a half years he had us ('sir' or 'miss'). He loved showbiz and card tricks - not easy to do when you're also fond of keeping your left hand in your blazer pocket. He also loved singing and was appreciative of ladies. On arrival each morning, he regularly paused at the top of the steps to salute Miriam and compliment her on her turn-out: "You're looking very smart this morning, Mrs Daniels."

Miriam, who always hated being called 'Mrs', would just as regularly shout at him: "You get to your classroom!" At which, Anthony would nod, smile, salute and do as he was told.

The atmosphere of Cowes Yachting Week that Anthony brought with him was delightfully heightened when Maureen brought a bag of chauffeurs' caps to school one day. Seeing its potential, Anthony seized the best cap and placed it on his head at a jaunty angle. I wanted to rush down the road to buy gin, tonic, ice and a lemon, but Miriam was looking and it was time to start work. Anthony wore the cap all day. He did his Maths and English in the saloon, went out on deck at playtime, took his lunch in the wardroom (I forgot to propose the Loyal Toast), and spent the afternoon below decks. He had a lovely day. He hurried into school the following day to repeat the process and go on another cruise but, the moment he had fixed the cap on his head precisely as he wanted it, Miriam told him to take it off 'at once!' She may have been envious, because later that day she wore it herself, but she didn't have Anthony's flair.

At heart poor Anthony was deeply confused. There were too many people in his life in substitute parental roles. What he lacked was someone of his own. What he wanted was his mother. The rest of us became blurred together in his mind into some kind of hermaphrodite corporate-carer. He once called for my attention by addressing me in rapid succession as "Miss, Uncle, Harry, Sir..." We were all part of his tragic drama, from which the leading player was missing.

As often happened with New Riverside children, Anthony chose the moment to voice his innermost sadness when his group was seated round the dinner table together, with Anthony sitting next to Ruby. She was spooning mashed potato on to the children's plates. He took the plate she offered him, and said: "Miss, I now know that there is no hope".

The hope that had disappeared from Anthony's life was that of ever seeing his mother again. This hope had provided him with a poor sustenance for most of his life. Adults - Miss or Uncle or Harry or Sir - had advised him that he should face the reality that in all probability his mother didn't want to see him (I think that was what Anthony's mother had told his social worker). For years Anthony had been unable to admit that to himself. He had continued to chew on a dream. He had known others for whom that dream had come true, characters in fairy stories and television dramas. That was the theme of almost every one of the blooming *Ladybird Much Loved Tales*. We all have dreams that are unlikely to come true. Anthony's case was perhaps different. To make his dream come true just one person had to change her mind. To have the strength and the courage to see that this wouldn't happen was as remarkable as it was painful.

Anthony left New Riverside on July 19th, 1979 when he moved to another children's home on the Sussex coast. I still regret that I was somewhere else that day.

22

After six years at New Riverside, it was time to think about moving on. Not having my own group meant there were no longer any children that I could consider mine. As Deputy Head, supposedly experienced and certainly paid more, I was the immediate higher authority called upon to deal with children *in extremis* or with the trickier situations. Sometimes - too often, I began to think - I was called in to back up decisions or attitudes taken by the group teacher, which I didn't agree with, which meant more acting. I always tried to manoeuvre child and teacher towards a negotiated settlement, but there were occasions when negotiations ended with teacher, child and me all dissatisfied. The group teacher wanted me to turn into a 'now just you listen to me' sort of teacher, but I was more the sort of 'let's sit down and have a quiet little chat' sort of teacher. It was a pity I didn't drink tea, because I could then have been a 'let's have a cup of tea' sort of teacher.

My shortcomings in this department were brought home to me by a young police officer one autumn morning at New Riverside when I was having a quiet little roving chat with a difficult lad who was threatening to leg it down the road. His name was Carl, he was only eight years old, and he hadn't been with us long. He had been referred for special education at the end of a long process that began after he had witnessed his mother being hacked to death with a machete by her boyfriend. On this particular morning, Carl had had a row with his teacher and was furious.

The young cop happened to be passing, heard me negotiating with Carl, and decided to shove his face in. He entered the school property - I should have told him to move along – and hung about for a few minutes, while I continued stalking and talking to Carl. Eventually, Carl went back into the school.

The young cop was not impressed. "Do I take it you're supposed to be a teacher at this school?" he said, and he made that upward and backward nod of the head that means "Cuh!" Maybe he was acting, but I fear not.

I was also not happy with the way Miriam was not happy with the new Deputy Warden of the hostel. He infuriated her, and there were Head-to-Deputy-Head arguments between them. The Deputy's name was Raymond, and he was adept at what you might call sleight-of-tongue. He was one of those people with whom what is supposed to be clarification becomes confusion. You start off talking about the work of Greenpeace, say, and after five minutes hear yourself saying something that sounds as though, horribly, you are advocating a return to capital punishment.

Relations between Miriam and Raymond worsened. She accused him of introducing practices that ran directly counter to the ethos of the hostel, which is a grandiose way of saying that he didn't do what he was told. She returned from meetings in the hostel scarlet faced, quivering with rage, threatening extreme action. This was potentially disastrous. Children in mainstream schools are hurt by rows between home and school and, to our twenty weekly boarders, hostel was home.

It was the psychiatric team who suggested Miriam and Raymond should meet every week at a fixed time. The idea was that this would prevent them meeting only when tempers were raised, and would allow them to discuss work before any sort of crisis had been reached. So it was decided that Miriam and Raymond should have a working lunch every Wednesday in Raymond's house. It was a reasonable plan, but there was never a hope of it succeeding with Miriam and Raymond. When they came together, something animalistic took place. I don't mean that hackles rose and teeth were bared, because I don't think Raymond had hackles, though I'm not sure about Miriam. It was more as though, the moment they got wind of each other, Miriam went into the attack and, though Raymond lay down submissively, Miriam just went on and on and on, snapping and snarling.

After a number of unproductive Wednesdays, the psychiatric team developed their original idea. They proposed I should join Miriam and Raymond at these working lunches, to witness what took place, to act as mediator, and to be available after the meeting if either of them wanted clarification on any of the points raised. In theory this, too, was a reasonable plan; in practice there was never a hope of it succeeding.

For several weeks I went over to Raymond's house at noon each Wednesday and sat at the table while he ate his lunch with Miriam sitting opposite him, arms folded, not eating hers. I said very little. Sometimes Miriam would ask me what I thought, and usually I didn't tell her, but made some bland and useless comment. It was awful. Raymond sat there, slowly forking pie and mash into his mouth, chewing miserably in silence, clearly having difficulty in swallowing, and then, after a few mouthfuls, tears would start trickling down his cheeks and into his little beard. I was profoundly grateful that he never turned his unhappy eyes in my direction. I think I would have burst into tears, which probably isn't what mediators are supposed to do. After 30 or 40 minutes of this, Miriam would announce that she had had enough, rise from the table and stomp back to school. I hovered about for a few seconds, in case Raymond wanted to say something. But he never did. He just sat there, tears still trickling, beard getting wetter and wetter, swallowing getting harder and harder.

"I'll see you later, Raymond," I would say, before following Miriam across to the school.

She was always waiting for me, and I always knew what she was going to say.

"You see! He's hopeless."

This may have been literally true, but I think she was using the word to mean 'worthless'.

"What am I going to do with him? I don't want him here. I don't like him."

I remember I used to spread my hands, expressively, as though I had something pretty wise to say, but all that came out of my mouth were platitudes, like 'I think he wants to do the right thing', 'I think he's perhaps confused', or 'I think he just needs time'.

Whatever I said, Miriam's response was always the same. "Oh, that's what *you* think, is it! Well, I don't. He's got to go."

She was determined, and Raymond did go. The Wednesday Lunch Club was mercifully dissolved. I don't know how it was arranged, but Raymond offered his resignation (I have images of him, sitting at the same table, tears trickling down as ever, while Miriam stands over him dictating his letter of resignation). Whoever wrote it, it was accepted. Raymond left. Another Deputy Warden arrived, with hackles. He stayed, and was successful.

But all this added to my feeling that it was time to go. Mary Evans had said that I should be looking for a Headship before I was forty. Such was my respect for her, and my desire to look good in her eyes, I decided that I should seek a headship. But first, I wanted a sabbatical from teaching. I applied to the

Institute of Education at London University for a place on their MA course in Child Psychology and Development, and to the ILEA for a year's secondment. I don't suppose there is an education authority in the land that now offers the deal that ILEA did then: a year on full salary with all fees paid. It was a far-sighted policy that enabled them to keep some of the higher flyers in education under their wing. I was never a high flyer, but I did flap my arms a lot.

In 1977, I was accepted at the Institute but denied secondment by the Authority. Even so, I felt my departure from New Riverside should be hastened. Either by getting a Headship or going on the Masters Course, or both, I would leave.

23

In January 1978, our son started at the Kent village school. The few villagers that still talked to us told us we were being foolish in sending him there. They sent their children to the Church of England Primary School in the neighbouring village, some four miles away; or, to put it more accurately, they drove their children there in big estate cars. They said that the neighbouring school was bigger and better. I have no idea what Bad Commies do, but Good Commies don't want their children to go to a Church school.

It should have been idyllic. Neighbouring Jacobean and Georgian cottages had been turned into a two class infant and junior school. Behind the fine buildings, fields ran down to the little river, beyond which a meadow climbed to a bluebell wood. The school had two classrooms, two teachers, and thirty children. What it lacked was equipment and inspiration. Unhappily, the two teachers who ran the school were not good enough for the children who went there. It took only two visits to the school and a series of brusque telephone calls from the Head teacher to convince Ruby our country days were numbered.

Fortune smiled. In March, one year after the disappointment of being denied secondment, I received a second letter from the Inner London Education Authority telling me all was well and I would be seconded from teaching for one year. I could start the course at the Institute of Education in that autumn. I handed in my resignation from New Riverside in May. I think Miriam was sorry to see me go. The Chair of Governors presented me with a blank envelope, the only contents of which were five £5 notes - no card, no letter. I don't remember much of my first last day at New Riverside (there were to be two other last days there). We had cakes and drinks in the staffroom once all the children had departed, and I was given a present. I made a short and slightly tearful speech.

In those last two terms, from January to July 1978, eight new children arrived at New Riverside and seven departed. Of those who left, three returned to mainstream school and four went out into the wide, wide world because they had reached school leaving age. I can't say I was sorry to say goodbye to Peter (the boy whose mum had stopped his father wetting the bed), but it was sad to lose three of the CSE group: Ian, Jayne and Trevor. I never saw Ian again, but a couple of times Ruby and I bumped into Jayne. She was well and happy, and was still in full-time education. Neither Ruby nor I realised it, but we were to see quite a lot more of Trevor.

In the Bad Old Days when I was child, it was held that everything that went wrong in school was the fault of children. They were not so much naughty as evil, spawn of the wicked Cain. Then came a period when blame was laid at the parents' door – it wasn't Cain after all, it was Adam and Eve. For some time now, teachers have been seen as the culprits – less Biblical in style but wicked in a lazy sort of way. The truth is that fault is immaterial when it comes to analysing the shortcomings of any educational system. It isn't so much 'who's to blame? ' as 'what shall we do about it?' Governments tend to get it wrong, starting with what they see as the desired end product of education, which is important, but not inspiring. The place to start is the beginning. No child sets out to be a failure at school. Even our children at New Riverside once had hopes that school would be a happy and empowering experience for them. It was our job and our privilege to rekindle that hope.

Looking at the list of children who came to New Riverside, I believe we may not have done much to help perhaps one third of them. Another third we helped enough for them to be happy and to manage their maladjustment. And at least a third made enormous progress. They learned to read and write and sing and paint and get on with each other, and they learned how to walk the tightrope strung across the dangerous arena of their own environment. Many went back to mainstream school; some should perhaps have stayed longer with us. Micky's stubbornness persisted, and brought his secondary school to its knees. Marianne's voice gave her secondary school a corporate headache - they should have let her sing more. Tom, too, stayed until school leaving age, got a job, married, and is now a father. I hope he'll love his family forever. Anita went to a High School in Croydon and we never heard what happened next. Sally, Miriam's tiny but doughty opponent, went back to the Junior School whence she had come to us - I hope they noticed a difference in her.

In 1971, the year New Riverside opened, there was a TV documentary called *Gale is Dead*. It was about a homeless young heroin addict who committed suicide in February 1970. Gale had been a pupil at a school run by Mary Evans, and Mary was interviewed for the film. Near the very end, Mary describes to Harold Williamson her last meeting with Gale in Charing Cross Hospital:

"She said to me, 'I shall die soon if I go on like this, Evans, shan't I'.

And I said, 'Yes, my love, you will'. And she shrugged her shoulders and said, 'Well, it doesn't matter now'. And I said to her, 'Well, you feel you haven't anybody really who wants you to live'. And she said,

'*That's it*'."

Mary then pauses for a beat, and says:

"*And she hadn't anybody, Mr Williamson*".

Perhaps something similar was true of my Leroy. We failed him. Maybe he had been too hurt, too damaged. Maybe we could never have helped him enough. It's possible. Against my wishes, Miriam sent him back to mainstream school too early - I think she was a touch afraid of the increasingly muscular teenage Leroy. He turned first to petty crime - crime of a more serious nature than raiding an ice-cream van - and was moved from mainstream school to a Community Home with Education in Bedfordshire. Here he found a good member of staff, who sadly had too little time to be of enough help before Leroy reached school leaving age. Once he hit sixteen there was no place for him in the Home. He returned to London, where there was no one to look after him, and set fire to a railway station. Much worse followed. He set fire to a house by pushing a teddy bear doused in petrol through the letter box and then throwing in a lighted match. Four people died in the flames. He went to prison for ten years. I visited him, wrote to him, tried to keep in touch. I last saw him 23 years ago. He had tracked down the father he never knew, who was then living in Canada. Leroy planned to join him. I still don't know whether he did or not, but a year ago, just after I began work on this book, he left a message on my website. It read: "Hi Nick, not sure if you remember teaching me at school? I was one of the naughty ones. Been trying to find you for years. Hope you will reply." Sadly, but perhaps predictably, he left no contact details. I have no idea where he is.

It is over 40 years since I first started at New Riverside. Most of the children I tried to teach are now in their late forties or fifties. Ruby and I married in 1981, and our son sent out the invitations to the wedding. Steve became a school inspector. Miriam died of cancer. Despite public protestation, the Inner London Education Authority was unforgivably axed by the Tories in 1989. Don't let us simply blame Thatcher. She wasn't acting alone in the bad things that were done. New Riverside is still where it was, and when I last heard, the roof still leaked.

I think about all the New Riverside children. I had dealings with hundreds of emotionally disturbed children in my seventeen years as a maladjusted teacher, but it's the first twenty or thirty of those children that Ruby and I still talk about most. They changed our lives. Dear old Barron used to say that children teach their parents how to be parents. Yes - I think they do. And maybe maladjusted children teach adults what an immense struggle it is to cope with life. What I *know* is, those first two years as a maladjusted teacher at New Riverside taught me almost all I know about trials and troubles, wants and needs, catastrophes and courage, fear, and love.

And I've never laughed, or cried, so much in all my life.

EPILOGUE

I once wrote that "the Seventies were essentially years during which the energy of the 1960s ran out, and millions of dreamers came back to earth with a bump". It wasn't true of me. I had never been a dreamer, and the years of great Social Mobility had seen me safely descend from Posh Boy to Pleb so smoothly that there was no bump when I met Ruby on her way up, and came to rest.

I stayed at New Riverside until 1980, when I became a Maladjusted Headteacher, but that is another Memoir…

NICK YAPP

Lightning Source UK Ltd.
Milton Keynes UK
UKHW041105200722
406121UK00004B/116